HIDDEN
HEALING

FOREWORD BY DR. IZABELLA WENTZ, PHARMD, FASCP
New York Times Best Selling Author of *Hashimoto's Protocol*

HIDDEN HEALING

A Nurse's Path to Overcoming Hashimoto's
and How You Can Too

Jasmine Parker RN, FMCHC

For more information, email jasmine@jasmineparkercoaching.com

ISBN: 979-8-89316-834-1 (Paperback)
ISBN: 979-8-89316-835-8 (Hardcover)
ISBN: 979-8-89316-833-4 (eBook)

In appreciation of your support and to thank you for being a valued reader, you can *download the Thyroid Lab Interpretation Guide for free!*

Simply, *scan the QR code* below and follow the instructions to claim your *free copy.*

DEDICATION

Dedicated to Samantha D'Amico, for being a
constant source of positive light in this world
and encouraging me to share my story!

*"You never know how or when you'll have an
impact, or how important your example can
be to someone else."* — *Denzel Washington*

CONTENTS

FOREWORD

asmine and I walked very similar paths – from an undiagnosed thyroid disorder to discovering functional medicine in the pursuit of answers, and ultimately, putting Hashimoto's into remission.

As autoimmune thyroid disorders become increasingly common, especially in women, we will continue to need trailblazers like Jasmine in the world of thyroid health. I call them "Root Cause Rebels" – the people who refuse to sit back and accept the conventional approach to thyroid care, who know that symptom management will never treat the root cause of the issue, and who stop at nothing to advocate for themselves and their health. They ask questions and dig for answers, they know that their symptoms provide important information about their health, and most importantly – they share what they learn, so that others don't have to go down the same path.

Jasmine takes us through her personal health journey, which finds her going from one specialist to another, given medications, and still never feeling better. This story is all too familiar – I experienced many doctors and specialists who couldn't tell me why I was experiencing symptoms, with some of them even telling me I was "just getting older" and others insinuating my symptoms were all in my head.

After working with thyroid patients for over a decade, I know that Jasmine and I are not alone. Unfortunately, this is the common experience of many people with Hashimoto's. Conventional medicine is sorely lacking when it comes to treating autoimmune disease, usually opting for symptom management rather than addressing the imbalances that cause the symptoms.

This is where functional medicine comes in. Functional medicine goes beyond symptom management and focuses on identifying the root cause of disease. It then aims to use lifestyle interventions like diet changes, stress management, gut healing, liver support, and supplementation to help bring the body into balance. Pharmaceuticals may also be used to support the patient while searching for and treating the root cause.

Discovering functional medicine was an important part of my journey towards remission from Hashimoto's, and Jasmine shares her experience with functional medicine and walks readers through the many factors that make up our health and functional lab testing that can help you identify your own unique root causes.

She then takes us through the key systems of the body that influence thyroid health and provides thorough information on what to consider and changes to implement for optimal thyroid support. She covers detoxification, gut health, nutrition, nutrient deficiencies, toxins, and mindset.

Hidden Healing is full of hope and profound insight into thyroid disorders, and exactly the kind of book I wish I had when I was struggling with my own mystery symptoms. Thank you, Jasmine, for sharing your story and inspiring Hashimoto's patients to be proactive in their healing journeys.

- Dr. Izabella Wentz, PharmD, FASCP
The Thyroid Pharmacist, New York Times Best
Selling Author of Hashimoto's Protocol

INTRODUCTION

or years, you have suffered from vague symptoms such as cold hands and feet, anxiety, stubborn weight, fatigue, thinning hair, and brain fog. You dismissed them until they became debilitating. Finally, fed up with the symptoms, you decide to discuss them with your doctor, only to be told that you are just anxious or stressed—reinforcing the notion that it's all in your head and nothing is wrong.

The next time you have a doctor's appointment, you bring up your symptoms again, hoping they will take a closer look and determine what's wrong. This prompts them to run some tests, but your lab results come back normal. The doctors tell you once more that nothing is wrong, reaffirming that it is all in your head, and advise you to stop worrying because nothing is wrong.

As time passes, your symptoms get worse because nothing has been done. Another doctor's appointment and your lab results are off the charts. You are diagnosed and are sent home with a one-size-fits-all treatment plan. GREAT! You finally have a diagnosis after all these years to get the magic lifelong pill that will make you feel better.

Later, you start to feel like crap again, and you lack the confidence to return to the doctor because you anticipate they will simply say, "Well, you have a thyroid disorder, so that's what your symptoms are from." At this point, they may run a few more tests and adjust your dosage in an attempt to alleviate your symptoms, but the relief is only temporary.

Inevitably, you are left wondering, *Is this it?* You have no education, resources, or tools to support you on this journey or to help you navigate your new diagnosis. Meanwhile, you feel defeated and burdened by the sad reality that there is nothing you can do to improve your thyroid health.

But what if I told you there is *more* to thyroid health than just the medication part, my friends? Thyroid medication can be a *great* tool in your toolkit, but what you may not know is that *you* control so much of your thyroid health outcome beyond medication.

With this book, I want to make you *aware* of the things in your control when it comes to your thyroid health. I want to *empower* you to take back control of your health and not let your situation or diagnosis control or define you. I hope to help you *discover* the holistic side of medicine. I hope to *encourage* you to seek healing. I want to *educate* you so you have a better understanding of just how much of an impact your thyroid has on your entire body and why it is so important to approach thyroid care with a whole-body approach. I hope this book provides you with education, resources, and tools to aid your healing journey.

The Merry-Go-Round

CHAPTER 1

Dark Clouds on the Horizon

"Just keep swimming" -Dory, Finding Nemo

The Initial Injury

*J*asmine, you have to wake up! Come on, wake up! Your alarm has gone off three times now! Wake up! I thought to myself, trying to muster up an ounce of effort to open my eyes. And then, my husband came in repeating the same urgent message: "Come on, you have to get out of bed, you have to leave soon."

I was a straight night nurse at a hospital in Minnesota, working twelve-hour shifts. By the time I got to shift five, I was exhausted and trying to hold on to every ounce of sleep I could get!

Okay, that was the extra nudge I needed to get up. I sleepily shifted in bed and began to sit up. I grabbed my pillow to place it behind my head, hoping to rest a few more minutes. As I threw my head back to hit my soft, fluffy pillow—WHACK!

My head rammed into the headboard. I winced in pain and held the back of my head for a few minutes until the pain subsided. Then, I made my way downstairs to grab some ice and ibuprofen.

I shrugged off the collision with my headboard and headed to work that night. After all, my head wasn't bleeding, and I wasn't disoriented, so there was no reason to stay home. I managed to get through the night without any problems and was looking forward to having the weekend off to catch up on sleep.

A couple of days later, I began to feel weird. My husband was in the kitchen making dinner and I was sitting on the couch in the living room, gazing in his direction.

"Are you okay?" he asked.

I started laughing hysterically. "Sh'yeah!" I stopped laughing and started gazing again.

"Are you sure?" he asked again.

I started laughing uncontrollably again. "Yes, yes, I'm okay." Then I paused and stared into space again. A part of me felt like I was acting strangely and that something was wrong, while the other part wondered if I was intentionally acting delusional.

He made his way to the living room with our dinner plates, sat down next to me, and asked, "What's going on?"

I started crying. "I have no idea, but something doesn't feel right," I said. I felt like I was a passenger in my body, who was aware of what was happening but not in control of it.

The next day, I had to schedule an appointment with my primary care doctor because things seemed to be getting worse. I couldn't stare at screens since my eyes hurt so much, nor could I tolerate any sounds because my head was pounding. My emotions were all over the place, and I spent most of the day sleeping due to exhaustion.

After explaining to the doctor about my little accident with my headboard and the symptoms that followed suit days after, she diagnosed me with post-concussion syndrome. She assured me that this would go away, but it would take a little bit of time. I had a stretch off from work coming up and decided to take advantage to rest up and heal. After all, it was a bump on the head, so it shouldn't take such a long time to get better.

During the following two weeks, I found myself enveloped in a suffocating darkness, shielding myself from even the faintest glimmer of light that dared to infiltrate my sanctuary. The sunlight filtering through the windows, the harsh glare of house lights, and the piercing brightness of electronic devices became sources of unbearable torment. To combat unavoidable sounds, I resorted to wearing headphones as a barrier against the daily noise, such as my husband's bustling morning routine or the unruly clamor of meal preparation. Each sound echoed like nails on a chalkboard, sending shivers down my spine. Amidst the oppressive darkness and relentless battle against sensory overload, my days blurred into a cycle of extended naps as my energy reserves were quickly depleted by the simplest activities.

Returning to work after two weeks, my sensitivity to sounds intensified. As I stepped back into the hospital environment, the incessant beeping of machines filled the hallways—a familiar yet grating sound to both patients and staff. Despite understanding the importance of these sounds for safety, their constant presence began to fray my nerves. It felt like being trapped in a nightmare of sound; no matter what turned off, another beep would soon follow, repeating endlessly. Clenching my fists, I felt a surge of helpless rage, often breaking down in tears from the relentless noise. The harsh glare from the computer screens compounded the discomfort, causing my head to throb incessantly. Seeking solace, I would retreat to an empty charting room or breakroom, turning off the lights even for a brief five minutes of peace and relief.

A few weeks later, as December arrived, the last night shift of my nursing schedule unknowingly heralded a pivotal moment in my life. I was transitioning into a period known as a "stretch off," a time when nurses typically work at the beginning of one week and at the end of the next, affording them a sizable break of six to eight days, depending on their contractual hours. During this stretch off, I found myself facing inexplicable distress. I suffered relentless daily panic attacks, each more suffocating than the last. Constantly, I was either hyperventilating, shedding tears, or experiencing waves of chest pain, nausea, tremors, and palpitations. The sensation of losing my grip on reality loomed ever closer, threatening to consume me entirely.

When the suffocating weight of anxiety and fear became too much to bear, I felt a desperate need to escape. I sought refuge in the comfort of family; my husband and I boarded a flight to Arizona, hoping to find solace and safety. I believed that the presence of family would act as a sanctuary, shielding me from the chaos that ensnared me, a beacon of hope in a sea of uncertainty. Despite the comforting distractions of sunny walks, tranquil lakeside moments, meditation, and the companionship of loved ones and pets, the grip of panic remained unyielding. I vividly recall the harrowing nights spent gasping for air, tears staining my cheeks as my husband attempted to soothe the storm within me. His voice, filled with reassurance and love, was a light in the darkness, yet the panic persisted, relentless.

As the days stretched on, the sense of hopelessness deepened, casting a shadow over our desperate attempts to find peace. The world seemed to close in around me, amplifying the sense of impending doom that haunted my every moment. Desperation and longing intertwined as I yearned for a respite from the unending cycle of panic and fear that had forged its way into my very being.

Another two weeks had gone by, and as our time in Arizona neared its end, anxious thoughts crowded my mind. They swirled with doubts and fears about the impending return to work. *I can't go to work like this. How am I going to deal with work? What am I going to do? I can't not work; we are in the middle of a pandemic. I need to help people!* I agonized, feeling the weight of responsibility pressing down on me. The urgency of helping others in the midst of a pandemic amplified the sense of duty that tugged at my conscience. Each day, a barrage of guilt clawed at my heart, reminding me of the patients and coworkers who relied on my presence. Echoes of uncertainty reverberated through my mind, questioning the fairness of my own struggles in comparison to others.

The doubts gnawed at me—how could I short my nursing unit by being absent when they, too, are enduring hardships? It has been a rough year for everyone! Why do I get a break? What if someone else is suffering more than I am? How is that fair? The weight of these questions bore down heavily, threatening to drown me in a sea of doubt and guilt. They clouded my mind, making it harder to find peace. I felt torn between my own well-being and the duty to support those around me, unsure of how to navigate the complex emotions pulling me in different directions.

My sweet, worried husband did not want me to return to work and I broke down in defeat. It was time to make the dreaded call to my boss and request a leave of absence. While one might assume that a leave would bring relief, for me, it was a daunting challenge—a painful admission of my struggles. The weight of failure and disappointment hung heavy on my heart. The panic and stress enveloped me, leaving me tossing and turning in restless sleep.

The following morning, nerves clouded my thoughts as I dialed my boss, only to be met with silence since he did not pick up. I left a voicemail filled with apologetic tones and a plea for time off, anxiously awaiting his response. When the phone finally rang, tears started streaming down my face. I hesitated to answer, giving myself one last chance to back out of my request. Taking a deep breath and wiping away the tears, I answered the phone. With trembling hands, I mustered the courage to ask for a leave of absence.

Unaware of the turmoil I had been going through, my boss expressed surprise and gently asked what had happened. Struggling to keep my composure, I managed to explain the distress I had been facing and how hard it had been to hold up when every part of me just wanted to break down. Then, in that vulnerable moment, his response had the power to transform everything. His words hung heavy in the air, penetrating the veil of self-doubt that had shrouded my mind.

"You're a nurse. We always put everyone else's needs above our own. It's what we do."

With those simple yet profound words, a newfound clarity began to dawn upon me. In that moment, I was struck by the realization that despite my own pain and suffering, I had been tirelessly devoting every ounce of my being to my nursing practice, for the sake of my team and patients. The idealized image I held for nursing, the self-sacrifice and unwavering dedication, had slowly been corroding my spirit from the inside out. It was a revelation that demanded a shift in my perspective, a call to find the delicate balance that had been sorely lacking. That turning point came when my manager voiced a sentiment that resonated deeply with me.

"I am here to support you and help you. Not just as a nurse in this hospital, not just as a nurse in general, but as a person."

In those words, I found the permission I had been seeking—the reassurance that it was not only acceptable but imperative to prioritize myself for once. With that realization, I understood that I, too, was a person deserving of care and consideration, just as important as those I had dedicated my life to serving. It was a transformative moment that marked the beginning of my journey.

Note: *Imagine that you work with a cabin crew of an airplane, and there's a pressure drop. Self-care is putting on your oxygen mask first before you try to help someone else put on theirs. If you don't take care of yourself first, you can't help everyone else.*

Upon our return home to Minnesota, I began meeting with my primary care provider almost every two weeks, anxiously awaiting her assessment. In response to my concussion scores, she referred me to speech, occupational, and physical therapy for evaluations. When I met with the speech therapist, she understood my struggles and made adjustments for my sensitivity, creating a safe space where it was okay not to excel at everything. This gesture stood out as a crucial reminder—especially for someone like me, driven by a relentless pursuit of achievement, where any perceived shortfall translated into personal failure—that no one is infallible. Despite my sluggish movements and overwhelming exhaustion, I pushed through the therapist's tests, ultimately securing clearance for my efforts.

However, I didn't feel the same sense of support during my interactions with the physical therapist. A warmth ran through my body as it dawned on me that I was not in a safe space. I felt frozen, holding back tears as she yelled, "What's your problem?" and I completely shut down. She rushed through the tests, and I remained completely silent, wishing for it to end as tears glossed my eyes. I fought to see through them and keep going. Her parting advice, tinged with impatience, demanded that I disrupt my long bouts of sleep and engage in physical activities. This only added to the weight of expectations and pressure already burdening me. The intersection of dismissive medical attitudes and self-imposed pressure to hasten my recovery and return to work formed a storm within me, one that threatened to engulf my fragile sense of hope and resilience.

Note: *You truly have no idea what people are going through, and we as a species tend to deal with a lot of life's ups and downs internally. Always lead with kindness and don't be assumptive or judgmental.*

As the weight of physical and mental exhaustion bore down on me, the last thing I needed was someone dismissing my struggles with a mere wave of their hand. If only it were that simple; if I could banish this overwhelming weariness with a thought, I would have done so long ago. The truth was, I wasn't choosing to be tired—it was a relentless companion that refused to be evicted. What she also failed to grasp was the paralyzing fear I felt, knowing that even the least stressful chore could unleash debilitating migraines. I couldn't afford to exacerbate my condition; the thought of regressing instead of progressing loomed over me like a shadow. Despite my reservations, all three therapists eventually granted me their stamp of approval, asserting that from their professional standpoint, nothing was amiss. The more providers that cleared me, the harder it was to shake off the unsettling feeling of my primary care provider's silent accusations whispering, *You must be faking it; this should be resolved by now.*

Note: *While it is incredibly easy to tell people to just do the damn thing and get out of your office, it is way more helpful and impactful if you ask questions to understand their situation, to be able to identify their barriers to your recommendations and help them navigate how they can overcome them to actually see results and get better.*

At some point, my primary care doctor was dumbfounded to see that my migraines still persisted. With no other recourse, she sought assistance from specialists. Thus began my journey with neurology to address my agonizing migraines. Upon my first visit to the neurology clinic, I was greeted with smiling faces and led to a consultation room for a detailed discussion of my symptoms and an eye exam. After the test, the doctor suggested that an occipital nerve block might do the trick. He explained that the procedure would entail six injections to the back of my head. Although the idea sounded daunting, he assured me that the needle would cause the least pain; it was the solution itself that might sting.

Despite the doctor's reassurance and his offer to take breaks, I was mortified at the thought of needles penetrating my head. I just wanted to get the procedure over with and hoped I would never need it again. I steeled myself, bracing for the discomfort as the injections began. With each prick, I focused on my breathing, willing myself to endure the ordeal. However, by the time the fourth injection pierced my skin, a wave of nausea and dizziness overpowered me, signaling that my body had reached its limit under the assault of pain. I raised my hand to signal him to pause.

Note: *I wouldn't recommend pushing yourself to your breaking point. Speak up for yourself if something is discomforting, uncomfortable, or making you feel ill. You are not being an inconvenience. There is plenty of time to get the task done. It is your body.*

After enduring the torment of six painful injections, I left the clinic exhausted, clutching a list of prescribed medications and a sheet detailing migraine-triggering foods. This list included common items like caffeine, alcohol, aged cheeses, chocolate, bananas, fermented foods, processed meats, and food additives. Many of these foods were staples in my normal diet, but at the time, I had not fully grasped how significantly they could contribute to migraines. Now, armed with these tools and feeling a glimmer of relief from the injections, I felt a surge of optimism as I embarked on this new treatment plan.

Living with migraines is an all-encompassing battle, marked by ceaseless pressure, relentless pain, and a yearning to detach my throbbing head from my body for any relief. I followed up with my neurologist over a series of monthly appointments in pursuit of a remedy. At each visit, I voiced my disappointment as the prescribed medications failed to bring relief, only to be met with assurances that finding the right solution was an intricate process, requiring patience. Despite the ongoing cycle of changing dosages and medications, my pleas seemed to fall on deaf ears. I felt misunderstood, and it seemed as if they blamed me, repeatedly emphasizing the importance of avoiding trigger foods and adhering to the medication regimen.

Despite my compliance, I found myself one day crippled by a debilitating migraine. Having exhausted all allowable medications, I lay curled up in a ball in the dark, tears streaming down my face, pleading for the pain and pressure to stop. *I just wanted someone to make it stop.* I couldn't live like this; I couldn't even open my eyes, as my head was pounding intensely. That night, my husband took me to the ER. I lay on the stretcher in the dark, covered by a blanket, closing my eyes and hoping I could somehow magically fall asleep and the pain would fade away. Finally, the ER doctor arrived, and my husband recounted our exhaustive journey of futile attempts to alleviate my suffering.

The doctor was visibly taken aback as he listened to our struggles and reviewed the array of medications I had been taking. He couldn't hide his sadness as he solemnly informed us that the very medications intended to provide relief might actually be triggering rebound headaches. Recognizing the severity of my pain, he administered a medication with sedative effects, which allowed me to drift into a merciful unconsciousness.

However, upon awakening the next day, a surge of anger and frustration gripped me. The medications I had faithfully ingested in hopes of finding relief had instead exacerbated my condition. This vicious cycle of worsening symptoms and side effects was a stark reminder that the path to healing had been fraught with setbacks, pushing me further away from recovery rather than drawing me closer.

As the days turned into weeks and weeks into months, the symptoms of my concussion finally began to wane. I felt immense joy as the clouds started to part. It was a relief to notice that I could once more tolerate sounds without flinching at every noise that reached my ears. The same went for light—I was finally able to tolerate it, and I no longer needed to find solace in darkness, hide under blankets, or nap frequently. Mentally, I found myself gradually more adept at handling stimuli without feeling overwhelmed within minutes, and the daily panic attacks ceased their assault. Thrilled with this progress, I sought my doctor's approval to resume work, albeit with certain restrictions in place. Though I harbored a quiet confidence in my ability to handle the workload without constraints, my doctor's insistence served as a stark reality check.

The first day back at work, two months later, proved to be a rude awakening. My resilience faltered within a mere two hours, succumbing to waves of head pressure, dizziness, and nausea. The disappointment festered within me, a bitter reminder of my brain's fragility and its prolonged struggle to function at its former capacity. *Why can't my brain just work right again?* I screamed internally. The fear of an uncertain future loomed large, casting shadows of doubt over my identity and purpose. Would I ever reclaim my role as a bedside nurse, a profession that had defined my entire existence? The prospect of losing this integral part of me sent shivers of despair down my spine, igniting a storm of self-criticism and unwarranted pressure to expedite my recovery. The ingrained notion of putting other people's needs before my own, nurtured over a lifetime, weighed heavily upon me, leaving me grappling with the unfamiliar concept of prioritizing self-care.

Note: *Understand that putting yourself first does not equate to selfishness but rather self-preservation. Your voice, your needs, and your well-being matter just as much as those of the people around you. You deserve care and compassion, too.*

Amidst the frustration with my health, the reassuring words of my doctor and husband held me steady. They reminded me that healing was a gradual process that demanded patience. With reluctant acceptance, I began to shift my focus to the delicate intricacies of my own mind—the very essence of my being that faltered in its recovery. Embracing their wisdom, I tackled my light-duty work with measured steps, one hour at a time, steadily nurturing my resilience and endurance. The initial progress was promising as I navigated the demands of my role, gradually increasing from four to six hours of dedicated time on light-duty tasks. However, as the months unfolded, a new chapter in my journey began, with unfamiliar symptoms manifesting, starkly different from the remnants of my concussion. *Why not add more fuel to the fire?* I thought as I faced these new challenges.

The Storm

One night, as I sat eating dinner with my husband, an inexplicable warmth crept across my face, igniting a fiery blush that spread down my neck and shoulders. Perplexed and alarmed, we swiftly began to search for answers, pondering potential triggers. Could it have been a stray morsel of food, or perhaps a side effect of medication? Despite stopping the prescribed medication, our concern persisted. A consultation with my primary care doctor yielded little resolution, as she attributed the reaction to a medication allergy. I wasn't convinced, as this diagnosis didn't align with my intuition. Determined to unravel the mystery of my sudden affliction, she referred me to a dermatologist. Upon entering the room, the dermatologist swiftly diagnosed the crimson hue on my skin as rosacea. She provided me with a tube of cream and concluded the consultation, leaving me adrift in a sea of unanswered questions.

Before that incident, in the quiet solace of my home, I was overwhelmed by fatigue and drenched in sweat, disturbed by the unsettling cadence of palpitations that thundered beneath my skin. I checked my pulse and discovered a resting heart rate soaring to staggering heights of 150 bpm, which climbed to 180 bpm with the slightest movement. Over the next couple of weeks, I kept a vigilant watch over my pulse. However, it was during the routine of light-duty work at the hospital, while seated at my desk among fellow nurses and doctors, that a potent cocktail of dizziness, chest pain, and sweating, punctuated by the eerie drumbeat of a racing heart, overcame me. Concealed behind a mask of composure, I weathered the storm in silence, bearing the weight of fear and uncertainty alone to shield my colleagues from the looming specter of panic.

I messaged my husband, who implored me to seek help in the ER. However, I was stubborn when it came to my own health and felt a lingering resolve to fulfill my duties. I teetered on the edge of indecision, my fate hanging in the delicate balance between duty and self-preservation. I decided to remain seated and hoped the symptoms would soon pass. As I clocked out, I saw my boss in his office. The thought crossed my mind to tell him what had happened, but I didn't want anyone to set me back. So, I turned the other way and headed toward the elevators to go home.

Note: *I don't recommend following in my stubborn footsteps here*

The intensity of the symptoms had subsided before I left, and I knew that if I no longer had symptoms, they wouldn't do anything for me downstairs anyway. I would be left waiting for hours to see someone just for them to tell me, "Nothing is wrong. Go home." Instead, I messaged my primary care doctor and informed her of the scary incident that had happened, and she arranged for me to wear a cardiac monitor for forty-eight hours. When the results came back, she stated that it was in fact a very high heart rate, but the rhythm was not dangerous, but she would like to put me on a prescription medication to bring my heart rate down. This would come to be the eighth medication I was put on since my concussion.

There was no investigation past this point for my sudden heart rate change which left me wondering even more what the hell was happening with me.

Now what?

By this time, I was sick and tired of being sick and tired. I was frustrated that no one could explain what was happening to me, nor did anyone seem to have the time to help me figure it out. I was exhausted from the endless rounds of doctor and specialist visits that ended with unanswered questions and a whirlwind of prescription medications, each with its own side effects. On top of my personal health struggles, an important work deadline was approaching—a stark reminder of the precarious balance between my health issues and professional responsibilities.

At this hospital, we nurses were given twelve weeks of light duty. Unfortunately, as time passed, a return to full duty was required. To continue working at the hospital and keep improving, I had to resume bedside duties after that period of light administrative work. Now, I was expected to perform at 100% with no restrictions. However, since my doctors hadn't fully cleared me, I was placed on a leave of absence again. At this point, I didn't know what else to do. Any progress I made seemed only to lead to new, frustrating challenges.

CHAPTER 2

The Shift

"We find the truth only when we are searching for it. Sometimes the truth may be right in front of our eyes, but we may not see it because that is not what we are seeking for." -Andre Gide

Months had passed in a blur of fleeting appointments, endless prescriptions, and daily battles with unexplained symptoms. Despite the array of medications prescribed to me, the answers remained elusive. I juggled visits to various specialists, each offering no more insight than the last. It seemed that no one could unravel the mystery of my ailments, much less provide a solution. Questions hung heavy in the air, unanswered and unspoken, as I grappled with the unrelenting uncertainty of my condition.

Trying to find a connection between my symptoms, I delved deeper into discussions with these medical professionals, only to be met with indifference and detachment. "Not my problem," they would say, passing the responsibility like a

JASMINE PARKER, RN, FMCHC

burdensome baton to the next in line. Frustration festered within me, a gnawing sense of abandonment and neglect in the face of my suffering. Doubts whispered insidiously into my mind—was I truly to blame for my own predicament? The fleeting moments spent in their presence each month could never capture the gravity of my daily battles.

Dismissed and disregarded, my anger simmered beneath the surface, a potent blend of frustration and desperation. The sting of being cast aside, deemed unworthy of attention and understanding, fueled a fire within me. The insistent drumming of my symptoms demanded recognition, a cry for help lost in the cacophony of dismissive professionals and impersonal diagnoses. I decided I would no longer allow their indifference to dictate my journey toward healing. Each dismissive remark and each callous shrug only served to steel my determination. For I was not a mere collection of symptoms to be brushed aside—I was a person, yearning for relief and understanding amidst the storm of confusion.

Later that week, in a moment of shared vulnerability, my chiropractor shared a personal story that ignited a spark of inspiration. I believed that if they could uncover that person's truth, surely there was hope for unraveling the complexities of my own symptoms. Her words resonated with me, instilling a newfound sense of hope and possibility in my heart. With a grateful nod, I resolved to take control of my own journey toward healing. Armed with the name of a Functional Medicine doctor she had recommended, I made an appointment, determined to explore a new path that promised answers and understanding. The prospect of reclaiming my health and vitality beckoned me forward, a glimmer of hope shining brightly on the horizon of possibility.

As the appointment day dawned, I found myself seated in the calm confines of the Functional Medicine doctor's office, anticipation fluttering in my chest. His demeanor was reassuringly composed, a stark contrast to the rushed consultations I had grown accustomed to. With a gentle prompt, he invited me to share the tumultuous journey that had led me to his doorstep.

Taking a deep breath, I recounted the tale of my head injury from the waning days of 2020, the gradual onset of debilitating symptoms, and the frustrating lack of answers from a myriad of doctors who had crossed my path. I presented him with the exhaustive list of symptoms that had plagued me for months now, a tangled web of physical and emotional distress that seemed to defy explanation. The doctor's expression remained contemplative as he paid rapt attention to the litany of symptoms I presented before him. To my astonishment, he did not rush to offer a quick diagnosis or prescribe yet another medication. Instead, he asked for a moment to think, a simple yet profound gesture that resonated deeply within me. In a healthcare system marked by swift assessments and hurried conclusions, his deliberate approach stood out as a beacon of genuine care and consideration.

Then, in a split moment of clarity, he uttered a term that reverberated through the room—thyroid disorder. The words cast a new light on my journey of uncertainty and frustration. A whirlwind of emotions swirled within me as I grappled with the unexpected revelation—how did a concussion lead to thyroid problems? The absurdity of the situation struck me, and laughter bubbled up from within, a release of tension and disbelief at the sudden twist in my medical odyssey.

Determined to validate his insights, I embarked on a journey of self-discovery. I ordered an at-home test for my thyroid levels. The results, when they came, spoke volumes, confirming the doctor's suspicions with undeniable clarity. Armed with this newfound knowledge, I went to my primary care doctor and presented the evidence of my elevated thyroid levels. My TSH was 25.45; normally, it was 0.6. At the time, in my location, the standard lab range for a TSH reading was 0.35–4.94, so I was definitely above normal. In that moment of revelation, a sense of relief and vindication washed over me…for a moment. Despite the tangible evidence of change laid out before her, my primary care doctor hesitated to pursue further testing for my thyroid. With a dismissive wave of her hand, she cited my previous thyroid results were normal and suggested that this was merely an anomaly attributed to stress.

In a moment of quiet resolve, I found my voice rising in gentle protest. This was not merely a passing concern or a momentary blip on the radar of my health. These symptoms were my reality, the invisible chains that bound me in a cycle of uncertainty and discomfort. With measured determination, I refused to accept her dismissive comments and insisted that she needed to thoroughly check my thyroid function. This was my body, my health, and I owed it to myself to seek the answers that had eluded me for so long. I stood my ground with a grace born of conviction, unwavering in my resolve to advocate for my well-being. In response to my voiced concerns, my practitioner reluctantly acknowledged them and agreed to order the full thyroid test.

Note: *Don't be afraid to advocate for your health and wellness. If something doesn't make sense to you or doesn't feel right, say something. If the plan doesn't align with you, collaborate to come up with one that does. It's your body; you ultimately decide.*

The moment of truth arrived as the results from the thyroid tests she had ordered finally came back. They showed a matching TSH level and also positive thyroid antibodies, painting a picture of a deeper imbalance within. The significance of these findings hung in digital silence, beckoning for a guiding hand to navigate the uncertainties that lay ahead. In her digital note, she offered a glimpse into the realm of autoimmune disorders, fraught with complexities and uncertainties. She reassured me that while the condition was not inherently dangerous, it could have a tangible impact on my quality of life. With a blend of caution and hope, she laid out the next steps on this journey of healing—an ultrasound of my thyroid and the initiation of thyroid hormone replacement medication.

Education Time

Let's take a hot minute to understand what exactly a thyroid is and its role in the body. We will also learn what hypothyroidism and Hashimoto's are, how they are diagnosed, and the treatment options available for them in the conventional medicine care model.

The thyroid, located at the front of your throat, is a part of the endocrine system. The endocrine system is a network of glands that includes the hypothalamus, pituitary, thyroid, parathyroid, thymus, adrenals, pineal, pancreas, ovaries, and testes. These glands create and release hormones into the bloodstream, which act like messenger molecules. They provide instructions to different parts of the body, ensuring that everything from organ function to tissue coordination runs smoothly.

Let's take a closer look!

The hypothalamus, a small yet mighty region in our brain, releases thyroid-releasing hormone (TRH), which stimulates the pituitary to release thyroid-stimulating hormone (TSH). TSH will then stimulates the thyroid gland to produce and secrete T4 (thyroxine), T3 (triiodothyronine), and calcitonin. This is a feedback loop! So when there is plenty of T4 and T3, the hypothalamus pauses the release of TRH, which then of course pauses the release of TSH. If we have enough, we definitely don't want more!

Naturally, if there is not enough T4 and T3, the hypothalamus tells the pituitary, and the pituitary in turn tells the thyroid to wake up and get to work! *Thyroid hormones are super important because they affect every cell and every organ in the body.* They regulate how your body uses energy, which can influence weight gain or weight loss, slow down or speed up your heart rate, and also affect the speed at which food moves through your digestive tract. Thyroid hormones also raise or lower your body temperature, affecting conditions like cold hands and feet or sensitivity to heat. Additionally, they control how your muscles contract, influence brain development, and control the rate at which your body replaces dying cells, crucial for skin and bone maintenance.

Now that you have a basic understanding of what a thyroid is and what it does, let's touch on what happens when things fall out of balance and how conventional medical care (our current healthcare system) treats the anomalies.

Hypothyroidism

According to the Cleveland Clinic, "Hypothyroidism occurs when your thyroid does not produce and release enough thyroid hormone into your body. This can be due to a primary cause, which directly affects the thyroid gland, such as Hashimoto's disease, radiation or surgical treatment for hyperthyroidism, iodine deficiency, inflammation of the thyroid (which can occur from viral illnesses or pregnancy), or a hereditary condition. Alternatively, it can result from a secondary cause, which means a failure somewhere in the feedback loop involving the pituitary gland and hypothalamus."

Testing

The primary method for diagnosing hypothyroidism is through a TSH blood test. If you have examined your lab results before, you may have noticed a reference range, which includes a high end and a low end. This reference range is determined by the "healthy" or "normal" population in your area. If your TSH level falls within the normal limits of this range, further testing is typically not required. However, if your TSH is outside the normal range, your healthcare provider may order additional thyroid lab tests, such as T4 and T3 tests, and sometimes thyroid antibody tests.

Blood Draw:

TSH- his indicates how much TSH is in the bloodstream. *TSH is a pituitary gland hormone that, when released, triggers your thyroid to release X amount of hormones (T3 and T4).* TSH level can vary throughout the day so getting your lab ran in the morning is best.

T4- is the main hormone the thyroid produces (80%), but it is *inactive, meaning it doesn't affect your body's cells until it's converted to an active form, T3. This conversion does not happen in the thyroid but* in the liver and kidneys.

- **T4 total**: This indicates bound and unbound T4 in your bloodstream.

- **T4 free**: This indicates unbound T4 available for use in the tissues.

T3- is the second hormone your thyroid produces (20%) and is the active form, meaning it impacts the cells in your body.

- **T3 total**: This indicates bound and unbound T3 in your bloodstream.

- **T3 free**: This indicates unbound T3 available for use in the tissues.

rT3- when T4 converts to T3 it can convert as T3 or reverse T3. The difference is reverse T3 *turns thyroid receptors off making it inactive.* Why does it do this? In response to stress! It is the bodies way of trying to save energy.

- **T3 reverse**: An inactive form of T3

TPO- is an enzyme found in the thyroid that helps with the production of thyroid hormones.

- **TPOAb**: Detected in 95% of people with Hashimoto's

TG- is produced by thyroid cells and aids the body in creating, storing, and releasing thyroid hormones. This lab can show the level of thyroid damage but, if elevated, can also *be an indicator of thyroid cancer.*

- **TGAb**: Detected in 80% of people with Hashimoto's

- **TG**: A protein made by the thyroid gland that helps guide thyroid cancer treatment. <20 ng/mL

Ultrasound – This test is utilized to detect any lumps or nodules.

Radioactive Iodine Uptake – This test requires you to swallow radioactive iodine, in a small amount, so it can be determined how well your thyroid is working. If your thyroid absorbs only a small amount of the iodine, it can point to hypothyroidism. If it absorbs a large amount, it can indicate hyperthyroidism.

Interferences

It is important that you understand there are certain medications and supplements that can interfere with your thyroid lab tests, thyroid function, and/or the thyroid's ability to absorb thyroid medication.

Can alter thyroid function and test results
- lithium
- amiodarone
- iodine or kelp supplements
- Immunomodulating drugs like interferon alpha and interleukin-2
- certain chemotherapy drugs
- tyrosine kinase inhibitors, like Nexavar (sorafenib) or Sutent (sunitinib)

Can get in the way of thyroid medication absorption
- calcium carbonate
- iron sulfate
- proton pump inhibitors like Prilosec (omeprazole) and Prevacid (lansoprazole)

Can interfere with lab measurements
- certain nonsteroidal anti-inflammatory drugs (NSAIDs)
- certain anticonvulsants
- heparin (a blood thinner)
- Lasix (furosemide)
- glucocorticoids (steroids such as cortisone)
- Isotretinoin
- biotin

Other things that can impact your thyroid test results are fasting (this includes overnight), stress, body weight, alcohol, smoking, diets high in processed foods, soy-based products, tea and coffee, and toxic exposure to lead, mercury, arsenic, pesticides, PFAS, and nitrate fertilizers.

Symptoms

Your thyroid symptoms are also important, but they can be challenging to pinpoint because they are often vague and can easily be dismissed or misdiagnosed. Additionally, these symptoms can develop slowly over many years. Your thyroid plays a role in numerous body functions such as metabolism, body temperature regulation, brain development, heart and breathing rates, digestion, mental activity, fertility, and the maintenance of skin and bones. Therefore, if it is not functioning optimally, you may experience symptoms such as the following:

HYPOTHYROID SYMPTOMS:
- numbness
- tingling
- anxiety
- depression
- gastrointestinal motility problems
- weight issues
- irregular menstrual periods
- fertility issues
- fatigue
- high cholesterol
- droopy eyelids or puffy face
- dry skin
- feeling forgetful

Treatment

When it comes to hypothyroid treatment, the number one approach is to start synthetic (man-made) thyroid hormone medication. The most commonly prescribed medication is Synthroid, or levothyroxine. Thyroid medication can be an amazing tool in managing your thyroid health. It may help you feel better symptomatically right away. However, it must be dosed correctly for each individual, and unfortunately, it is often not.

A large study followed 162,369 patients with hypothyroidism over 23 years and revealed that 11.6% (approximately 18,000 people) of the TSH values achieved were indicative of overtreatment with medication, while 32.4% (approximately 52,000 people) suggested undertreatment. Therefore, if thyroid medication is part of your treatment plan, it's crucial not to neglect regular lab tests to evaluate your correct dosage. If your dosage is not precisely adjusted, you may continue to experience symptoms.

Barrier/challenge to getting the right dosage: It may be difficult to get the appropriate dosage if you don't attend follow-up appointments or your provider does not educate you on the importance of follow-up visits and how they're indispensable for getting your dosage right.

Many people who are prescribed thyroid medication do not take it correctly. However, it potentially can be hard to fault them entirely because one cannot act on information they have never received. Or sometimes, details shared by pharmacists can be forgotten, or the person dispensing the medication may not be thoroughly knowledgeable about the topic. At other times, patients might disregard the medication instructions and start taking it on their own terms. There are numerous reasons why mistakes can happen. But I must remind you that taking the correct dosage of Synthroid is crucial, as both excessive and insufficient amounts can have effects on "growth and development, heart function, bone health, reproductive function, mental health, digestive function, and changes in blood sugar and cholesterol metabolism", according to the maker's of Synthroid, let's go through some important safety reminders:

Synthroid Medication Safety

- Synthroid should be taken on an empty stomach at the same time every day, ideally in the morning, about 30-60 minutes before eating.

- Do NOT abruptly stop this medication.

- Foods like grapefruit juice, walnuts, soy, high-fiber diets, iron supplements, calcium supplements, aluminum hydroxide found in some antacids, sucralfate, and prevalite can affect Synthroid's absorption.

- Thyroid hormones, including Synthroid, should not be used alone or in combination with other drugs to treat obesity or weight loss.

- In patients with normal thyroid levels, doses of Synthroid used daily for hormone replacement are not helpful for weight loss. Larger doses may result in serious or even life-threatening events, especially when used in combination with certain other drugs used to reduce appetite.

- Do not use Synthroid if you have uncorrected adrenal problems.

- Partial hair loss may occur during the first few months of taking Synthroid.

Table adapted from AbbVie. Synthroid. AbbVie, 2022.

Note: *If you thought you just needed to get to the right dose and you're set for life, I am afraid that is not true. Your dosage needs can change over time, depending on lifestyle factors, pregnancy, or weight gain/ loss. This is why it is important that you continue to stay up to date on your thyroid lab checks.*

Now you know what the hypothyroid treatment is, but have you and your doctor identified what *your* cause is? Is it the autoimmune disease Hashimoto's (most common in developed countries), iodine deficiency (more common in underdeveloped countries), congenital, pregnancy, a viral illness, treatment of hyperthyroidism, or a problem with your pituitary? For me, it was the autoimmune disease Hashimoto's!

Hashimoto's

According to the Cleveland Clinic, Hashimoto's is a lifelong autoimmune condition that can cause hypothyroidism. It affects five in one hundred people in the United States. Although anyone at any age can develop Hashimoto's, it is most commonly diagnosed between the ages of thirty and fifty, and women are ten times more likely to develop it than men. In an autoimmune condition, the body's immune system attacks its own cells and organs. In the case of Hashimoto's, the immune response targets thyroid tissue. The large number of white blood cells that accumulate in the thyroid leads to inflammation, which, over time, can damage the thyroid and impair its ability to produce thyroid hormones, resulting in hypothyroidism. Hashimoto's is diagnosed based on clinical symptoms of hypothyroidism, thyroid lab test results, and the presence of TPO antibodies.

Symptoms

Symptoms of Hashimoto's are a lot like those of hypothyroidism: a puffy face, memory problems, fatigue, weight gain, cold hands/feet, dry skin, depression, infertility, decreased sex drive, irregular menses, joint stiffness, and a slower-than-normal heart rate. However, the tricky part is that Hashimoto's can also have symptoms like those of hyperthyroidism: panic attacks, fatigue, difficulty sleeping, hair loss, irregular menses, a fast heart rate, and irritability.

Testing

Besides looking at the symptoms, diagnosing Hashimoto's is done through testing. As I mentioned above, if you are suffering from these symptoms, a blood lab test for TSH is the standard to run. If that is abnormal, then your provider will check your T4 and T3 levels, and if these are off, they may run thyroid antibody tests to determine if Hashimoto's is the cause of your hypothyroidism. In some cases, your doctor may order an ultrasound of your thyroid to check if it is underactive or overactive, as well as if there are any growths such as tumors, nodules, or cysts.

Treatment

The treatment for Hashimoto's in conventional medicine typically does not address the immune system imbalance directly. Instead, it often focuses on determining whether clinical hypothyroidism is present. If your Hashimoto's results in hypothyroidism, the standard treatment involves taking synthetic thyroid hormone medication, similar to the treatment for hypothyroidism alone. However, if you do not have hypothyroidism but have elevated antibodies indicating Hashimoto's, your provider is likely to monitor your levels rather than start thyroid hormone medication immediately.

In future chapters, we will talk about why sitting and waiting in this stage can impact you negatively, as well as why the immune system needs to be addressed in Hashimoto's care.

Whoo! That is a buttload of information for anyone to intake. Let's just take a break here.

Oh, wait, that's right! I had a decision to make! Well, I personally decided to...

How Functional Medicine Saved Me

CHAPTER 3

Connecting the Dots

"Your body holds deep wisdom. Trust in it.
Learn from it. Nourish it. Watch your life
transform and be healthy." -Bella Bleue

Ipersonally decided to...*not start with thyroid medication*. This was a very personal decision, and I don't advise anyone to blindly follow my personal decision because you have to do what is right for *you* and your unique situation. For me, I felt connected with the doctor who took the time to put the puzzle pieces together and figure out that I had an autoimmune condition. I wanted to work with him and had complete faith that he was the guy to help me get to remission and stay in control of it.

Note: *When it comes to making healthcare decisions for yourself, make sure you know all your options and have enough information about them, so when it's time to make a decision, you can make the best one possible for you. After all, it is you who has to bear all the symptoms, side effects, treatments, and changes.*

If you choose to start with an unconventional route, like I did, you should expect most people to get upset or argue with you. This is because they don't *see* any other options, they don't *understand* your decision, and they are worried about the outcome, especially since they are not in control of making the decision for you. I decided that my life was not going to be controlled by medication or my autoimmune disease. Instead, I was going to take control of my health moving forward. It all started with filling out comprehensive client forms.

When visiting a healthcare provider, it is common practice to complete new patient health history forms. These forms are designed to capture vital information about your current health status, family medical history, allergies, vaccination records, social background, surgical history, and medications in use. Each section of these forms plays a crucial role in building a comprehensive profile of your health, contributing to the creation of your medical record. This record serves as a fundamental resource for healthcare professionals, offering insights into your health trajectory and aiding in the decision-making process for treatment strategies, diagnostic procedures, and necessary follow-up visits. By diligently providing accurate and detailed information on these medical history forms, you are actively participating in the collaborative effort to understand your state of health and facilitate optimal care and monitoring tailored to your individual needs.

When I scheduled an appointment with my Functional Medicine doctor, I anticipated the usual routine of filling out new client forms. However, I was pleasantly surprised to find that the health forms in Functional Medicine delved much deeper than I had previously experienced. Throughout this chapter, we will explore some of these "oddball" form questions. As someone with a keen interest in science and medicine, I welcomed the opportunity to explore a more comprehensive set of forms. Each question seemed to peel back another layer of understanding, providing me with new insights as I completed them. The thoroughness of these forms gave me a sense of reassurance; it was clear that the goal was to leave no stone unturned in uncovering any potential clues or connections that could lead to a resolution. These forms left no aspect of my health untouched. In essence, this comprehensive approach felt like a fresh start—an opportunity to lay the foundation toward understanding and addressing the root causes of my health concerns.

FM Health Forms Explored:

- birth and childhood history
- stress levels
- relationships
- family dynamics
- social support
- spiritual wellbeing
- career satisfaction
- environmental influences
- physical activity habits
- nutritional status through food journaling
- brain assessments
- metabolic evaluations

Note: *Everything you have experienced or been exposed to, from the time you were born to today, has impacted your current state of health.*

At the time, I couldn't quite grasp how all these personal questions about my life could provide insights into my health crisis and lead to a solution. Why did it matter if I attended church or how my home environment influenced my well-being? What relevance did my job satisfaction or past traumas have to my current health issues? The truth is, every aspect of our lives is intricately connected to our health. By unraveling these seemingly unrelated threads and analyzing them through the lens of Functional Medicine, we can uncover valuable clues that may hold the key to resolving health challenges. Let's break it down.

Your Beginning

When a baby is born naturally, it is introduced to helpful bacteria from the mother's body, which is crucial for establishing the baby's gut microbiome—a special community of bacteria that influences many aspects of health through its interactions with various body systems. These bacteria impact the immune system, nervous system, and endocrine system, while also assisting in functions like digestion. In a C-section birth, the baby misses out on this initial contact with the mother's bacteria.

After birth, the baby is nourished either by breastfeeding or formula feeding. Breast milk provides special nutrients like long-chain fatty acids that support eye and brain development, as well as enzymes, hormones, and immune substances that help protect against infections. These benefits are not found in formula feeding.

This leads us to the next question: Were you sick a lot as a child? Did you experience frequent respiratory illnesses, ear infections, or stomach bugs? Research indicates that those who were formula-fed had double the risk of developing ear infections, were 3.6 times more likely to contract lower respiratory infections, and were 2.8 times more likely to develop gut infections. This is because breast milk provides special protections against harmful germs present in the mother's environment, including dangerous pathogens such as *H. influenzae, S. pneumoniae, V. cholerae, E. coli,* and rotavirus.

If you were frequently sick as a child, perhaps you received antibiotics. If so, those also had an impact on your gut microbiome. While antibiotics are instrumental in eliminating harmful bacteria, they can also disrupt the balance of beneficial bacteria in the gut. This imbalance can impact vital functions that the gut microbiome contributes to, like digestion, metabolism, vitamin production, defense against other pathogens, and regulation of the immune system and inflammatory responses. Recovery of the gut microbiome following antibiotic treatment is a slow and incomplete process, often taking years for full restoration.

In summary, from the very beginning of *your* existence, your gut microbiome has been shaped by your early life experiences and environment, influencing your immune system and overall health as you continue to age and encounter new exposures.

Trauma

Ah, that six-letter word that everyone avoids, shoves away, locks up, and hopes to forget: trauma. Sadly, we all carry some form of trauma, whether big or small. Just the mention of the word can trigger uncomfortable memories, leading to an uneasy feeling in our stomachs. Believe me, I understand; I have faced my fair share of trauma in my life, both emotional and physical. It is a tough thing to confront. It can feel shameful, and the triggers can be overwhelming because you just want to forget.

Dealing with trauma requires considerable courage and bravery to acknowledge that you need help to process what happened, handle triggers, and learn how to let go. It takes even more courage and bravery to walk into a therapist's office and talk about it, reliving those painful moments. For me personally, choosing therapy was the best decision I ever made, but it wasn't easy. Healing takes time, but eventually, I reached a point where I could release the pain and feel truly free.

Your mind can be a very dark and scary place. It can feel like the world is ending or as if everything bad always happens to you, making life seem unfair. If you feed this narrative, it grows. Truly, scientifically, what you think affects how you feel. Dwelling on negative thoughts leads to negative feelings, while focusing on positive thoughts can make you feel happier. Albert Einstein once said, "You cannot solve problems with the same kind of thinking used when you created them"—and he was absolutely right! For example, if you are constantly beating yourself up and become your own worst critic, who is left to offer you love and support? Who tells you everything is okay? It certainly isn't you, friend. To support and encourage yourself, you need a different mindset and approach, not one mired in constant self-loathing.

By avoiding these feelings, we are not letting go of them. Instead, they get stored inside us and can affect our health and well-being. Many people do not realize the connection between their emotions and the physical symptoms they experience. This lack of awareness often leads them to overlook their emotional needs while focusing solely on physical complaints. It becomes even more challenging when individuals believe their symptoms are the sole problem, especially when medical tests show no apparent issues. This can leave them feeling invalidated, unheard, and unseen, exacerbating their existing feelings. This situation highlights the importance of treating the body as a whole, which involves acknowledging and addressing past experiences, including trauma. Understanding how these experiences impact not only our emotional well-being but also our physical health is essential.

Studies have found a strong link between traumatic experiences, especially those from childhood, and long-lasting health issues. These health problems can show up as different physical conditions.

Common physical disorders and symptoms

- somatic complaints
- sleep disturbances
- gastrointestinal disorders
- cardiovascular disorders
- neurological disorders
- musculoskeletal disorders
- respiratory disorders
- dermatological disorders
- urological problems
- substance use disorders

When someone experiences a tough situation or event, it can trigger changes in how their body reacts to stress. These changes may affect mental health, potentially leading to conditions such as PTSD. Additionally, these adjustments can impact the functioning of specific brain regions, such as the limbic system, and alter how the body manages stress hormones like cortisol.

Let me explain.

Our bodies have a built-in defense system that involves the activation of the sympathetic-adreno-medullar (SAM) axis, the hypothalamus-pituitary-adrenal (HPA) axis, and the immune system. When we sense danger, the body sends out signals to prepare for a potential threat. It releases adrenaline, also known as epinephrine, which boosts energy levels by releasing glucose. If the danger persists, the body then releases cortisol. Ideally, once the danger passes, these stress hormones should decrease as well. Our bodies respond to various internal and external triggers that can activate a stress response. However, if we are constantly stressed or feel unsafe, the stress hormones remain active, causing harm over time. Continuous high levels of stress can lead to damage, as noted by Harvard University. Excessive adrenaline can harm blood vessels and increase blood pressure, elevating the risk of heart attacks and strokes. Similarly, elevated cortisol levels can lead to physical changes and contribute to weight gain by promoting the accumulation of fat tissue.

Note: *If weight is on your 'problem' list, stress must be talked about!*

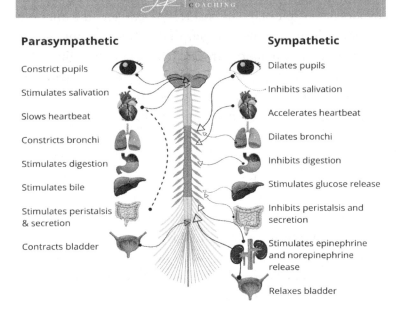

Parasympathetic   **Sympathetic**

Constrict pupils   Dilates pupils

Stimulates salivation   Inhibits salivation

Slows heartbeat   Accelerates heartbeat

Constricts bronchi   Dilates bronchi

Stimulates digestion   Inhibits digestion

Stimulates bile   Stimulates glucose release

Stimulates peristalsis   Inhibits peristalsis and
& secretion   secretion

Contracts bladder   Stimulates epinephrine
                                             and norepinephrine
                                             release

                                             Relaxes bladder

Support

In discussing friends, family, or spiritual life, the recurring theme is *support*. Social support has been shown to promote health by enhancing an individual's coping mechanisms, overall well-being, and resilience during times of stress. This is crucial when embarking on significant lifestyle changes or adjustments, which often come with various challenges and barriers. Some obstacles are self-imposed due to limiting beliefs such as "I can't," "It's impossible," or "This isn't for me." Other barriers may be financial, physical, mental, emotional, or time-related.

Having a support system is crucial during difficult times. Rather than facing negative experiences alone, seeking help can significantly improve your mindset and ability to overcome obstacles. In times of struggle, having someone or something to turn to for assistance can be uplifting. This is important because, as the saying goes, "Whether you think you can or think you can't, you're right!" Sometimes, it's hard for us to recognize our own capabilities, and a support system can help you stay committed, be consistent, and remind you why you are pursuing change. Support can come in various forms, including emotional, informational, financial, or practical assistance, and it can stem from a diverse range of sources, such as mentors, therapists, parents, friends, colleagues, or community groups. The key is to recognize whether you have a support network available. If you find yourself without support from family, friends, work colleagues, neighbors, or community groups, it may be tougher to handle health and emotional challenges, as these are often too overwhelming to manage by oneself.

Lack of support can significantly impact one's health challenges. As noted by Dr. Cole, "Feeling disconnected from the community can alter one's perception of the world. Chronic loneliness can lead to feelings of threat and mistrust toward others, triggering biological defense mechanisms. Loneliness can also serve as a catalyst for various health issues. It may accelerate the development of artery plaque, promote the growth and spread of cancer cells, and influence immune system responses, which in turn increases inflammation."

Self-Care

Self-care involves dedicating time to activities that enhance your physical and mental well-being. Do you struggle with prioritizing your needs over those of others? Do you often feel guilty or undeserving when you take time for yourself? Perhaps you believe you are not worthy of breaks, kind words, or nice things, which leads to self-imposed pressure and a habit of putting others first. Many of us find it challenging to place our needs above those of others, often neglecting our well-being in the process. Consistently prioritizing others sends a message that our own needs are insignificant. Self-care is essential as it helps manage stress, reduce the risk of illness, and boost energy levels. By examining how you approach self-care, you gain insight into your self-perception and your ability to prioritize your health.

Note: *Are you slaving you or serving you?*

Brain Assessment

Have you ever had a concussion or worse head injury?

Brain assessments are invaluable in identifying specific areas of difficulty within each brain region. Often, after experiencing a concussion, we tend to simply wait until the head feels better before resuming routine activities- be it sports or work. But head injuries, like concussions have an impact beyond the brain. Meaning the initial injury (act one) has repurcussions (act two) that affect organs like the gastrointestinal (GI) tract.

In Dr. John Bartemus 2020, International Best Selling book, *The Autoimmune Answer,* he states "a mild concussion has the potential to activate an immune response in the brain that is greater than mild; and just because someone no longer feels dizzy or nauseous, and can follow a pen doesn't mean the immune and neuroinflammatory effects of the head trauma have resolved. The consequences of a head injury aren't imprisoned in your skull, they are systemic"(82-83).

Since your head injury(s), *do you find that you now suffer GI symptoms/complaints/diagnosis or food sensitivities?* Perhaps your brain injury has never fully been healed.

You see the brain and the gut are connected and influence each other via the gut-brain axis. Research shows that head injuries can impact intestinal function and gut microbiota as well as contribute to the development of leaky gut, in as little as 6 hours post injury.

In my case, this assessment was a huge connection piece because it was my concussion that set off his storm. My concussion lead to leaky gut, which, in combination with a genetic predisposition and various triggers, awakened an autoimmune attack.

Note: *this is why taking a whole-body approach to your health is important. As I said before, everything that has happened to you in your life, has influenced your state of health. Some of those symptoms don't seem so out of the blue anymore huh?*

Nutrition

If your doctor asks about your nutrition, would a simple "good" or "fine" really suffice? One-word responses do not provide enough insight into this critical aspect of your health. Keeping a food journal is essential because we often cannot remember what we have eaten, the quantities of specific nutrients consumed, or how we feel after meals. By monitoring these details, you can gain deeper insights into symptoms like bloating, gas, heartburn, diarrhea, constipation, headaches, and skin issues. These symptoms could indicate challenges such as difficulties digesting proteins or fats, low stomach acid, leaky gut, food sensitivities, or blood sugar dysregulation. Furthermore, our diet affects the growth of beneficial or harmful bacteria in the gut, which can lead to various symptoms if an imbalance occurs. Research also suggests that the Standard American Diet (SAD) may contribute to chronic pain through persistent immune system activation.

By delving into these personal aspects of our lives, Functional Medicine practitioners aim to take a holistic approach to health, recognizing that true wellness encompasses not just the physical body but also the mind, spirit, and environment. Each piece of the puzzle contributes to the overarching picture of health and provides valuable guidance in crafting a personalized plan for health and restoration. As for the rest of the information, we test!

CHAPTER 4

A Deeper Dive

*"Without laboratories men of science are
soldiers without arms." -Louis Pasteur*

t wasn't until I underwent testing that the truth about
my thyroid disorder was revealed. With the right
tests, we uncovered many imbalances, and suddenly,
the bigger picture became clear, pointing us in the right
direction to address the root cause of the problems instead
of merely masking the symptoms. Elevated TSH and TPO
antibodies served as clear indicators of a thyroid autoimmune
problem. Furthermore, the results of my GI-MAP™ were
eye-opening, showing not only an *H. pylori* infection but
also other inflammatory bacteria wreaking havoc in my gut.
They also identified an immune system response, a gluten
reaction, and elevated beta-glucuronidase. Additional testing
unveiled a cascade of issues—from EBV to heavy metals like
cadmium and butene. In essence, a combination of genetic
predisposition, triggers, and a leaky gut created the perfect
storm for my autoimmune condition to awaken. You're

probably wondering at this point *"what the heck are all these tests"* - let's dive in and explore these tests and what they mean!

Test #1: Full thyroid panel

A full thyroid panel provides a comprehensive assessment of thyroid function by measuring levels of thyroid hormones, thyroid-stimulating hormone (TSH), and various antibodies associated with thyroid disorders. While standard lab tests often focus primarily on TSH levels, it's important to recognize that TSH, which is produced by the pituitary gland to signal the thyroid to release hormones T3 and T4, is just one component of overall thyroid health.

Relying solely on the TSH test may not provide a complete picture of thyroid hormone levels in the body. That is why it is essential to conduct a full thyroid panel, which includes tests for TSH, T3, T4, and TPO/TG (thyroid antibodies). By running this full panel, you can gain a better understanding of the overall health of your thyroid and make more informed decisions about treatment and management.

Thyroid-stimulating hormone (TSH)

This test is the primary thyroid test run, as TSH changes can occur before the actual thyroid hormone levels become too high or too low. A high TSH can signal that the thyroid gland is not making enough thyroid hormone (HYPOthyroidism), whereas a low TSH can signal that the thyroid is producing too much thyroid hormone (HYPERthyroidism). In addition to primary hypothyroidism, there is secondary hypothyroidism, which is signaled by a low TSH, possibly indicating an abnormality in the pituitary gland (the gland that releases TSH).

Triiodothyronine (T3)

This test in particular is favored more for hyperthyroidism diagnosis assistance because in hypothyroid patients, T3 is usually normal. This is because it is the last test to become abnormal, which could cause a delay in the diagnosis and treatment of hypothyroidism.

Thyroxine (T4) + Triiodothyronine resin uptake (T3RU)

The T4 test measures both unbound and bound T4 hormones. However, it cannot distinguish whether changes in T4 levels are due to variations in thyroid-binding globulin (TBG) levels or actual production issues by the thyroid gland. This ambiguity could mistakenly suggest a thyroid problem when there might not be one. To better understand the underlying causes, it is advisable to combine the T4 test with a resin uptake (T3RU) test. The T3RU test helps determine the activity of TBG in the body. By analyzing both tests together, healthcare providers can determine if changes in T4 levels are due to alterations in TBG levels. For example, if someone has elevated TBG leading to high T4 levels, their T3RU would typically be low. Conversely, if someone has low TBG and correspondingly low T4 levels, their T3RU would be high.

Free T4

This test measures unbound T4 hormones, providing a more accurate assessment because it directly evaluates the amount of T4 in the body without interference from other factors, such as TBG. This approach offers a clearer and more precise understanding of a person's thyroid health.

Reverse T3 (rT3)

In addition to standard thyroid tests, more advanced assessments like the reverse T3 (rT3) test are available. Although not commonly used in routine clinical practice, this test offers valuable insights in specific scenarios. For example, the rT3 test can be crucial in diagnosing hypothyroidism that may be complicated by concurrent drug therapies, such as amiodarone, which is high in iodine, or in cases of consumptive hypothyroidism. Additionally, studies have shown that the ratio of T3 to rT3 correlates with markers of insulin resistance, issues in converting T4 to T3, non-thyroidal illness syndrome, carbohydrate deprivation due to starvation, and bodily stress responses.

The thyroid primarily produces T4 (80%) and a smaller amount of T3 (20%). However, T4 must be converted into active T3, a process that can be hindered by various factors, including stress. The adrenal glands, which are part of the endocrine system and regulate the stress response, can impact this conversion. In times of stress, T4 may instead be converted into rT3, an inactive form of the hormone.

Thyroid peroxidase antibodies (TPOAb)

Thyroid peroxidase (TPO) is an enzyme produced by your thyroid gland. Normally, antibodies defend against foreign invaders. However, TPO antibodies are produced when the body mistakenly identifies TPO as a foreign invader and begins attacking it. While some individuals may test positive for TPO antibodies without showing symptoms of hypothyroidism, it's important to note that the presence of TPO antibodies can increase the risk of developing hypothyroidism in the future.

Thyroglobulin (TG) and Thyroglobulin antibodies (TGAb)

Thyroglobulin is an important tumor marker for differentiated thyroid carcinoma (DTC) following treatment. Additionally, thyroglobulin antibodies (TGAb) serve as a marker for thyroid autoimmunity. Primarily, TGAb is used to ensure the reliability of the thyroglobulin test during follow-up examinations in individuals with DTC.

According to Dr. Izabella Wentz, PharmD, FASCP, who is a clinical pharmacist, New York Times bestselling author of Hashimoto's Thyroiditis: Lifestyle Interventions for Finding and Treating the Root Cause, and pioneering expert in lifestyle interventions for treating Hashimoto's thyroiditis, the *optimal* reference ranges for these lab tests are as follows:

- **TSH**: 0.5–2 µIU/mL

- **Free T4**: 15–23 pmol/L

- **Free T3**: 5–7 pmol/L

- **Reverse T3**: 11–18 ng/dl

- **TPO antibodies**: < 2 IU/mL

- **TG antibodies**: < 2 IU/mL

Hashimoto's disease is typically diagnosed by evaluating symptoms of an underactive thyroid along with the presence of TPO antibodies. Interestingly, these antibodies can exist in the body for several years before they begin to affect hormone levels, often requiring a perfect storm of factors. For an autoimmune condition like Hashimoto's to manifest, three elements must be present: a genetic predisposition, external or internal triggers, and a leaky gut. The next test we discuss is designed to identify potential pathogenic triggers and evidence of a leaky gut.

Test #2 : GI-MAP™

Your gut bacteria not only support your immune system; they also play a role in thyroid function. Considering that up to 70% of your immune system is linked to gut health, it is crucial to address this when discussing immunity. According to Evexia Diagnostics, the "GI-MAP™ (GI-Microbial Assay Plus) test quantitatively assesses a patient's microbiome, focusing on bacterial, parasitic, and viral pathogens that can cause disease, disrupt microbial balance, and contribute to chronic gastrointestinal illness. The GI-MAP™ test is also a valuable tool for looking at intestinal health markers like digestion, immune response, and inflammation."

Some pathogens in the gut, such as parasites, small intestinal bacterial overgrowth (SIBO), Candida, *H. pylori*, and Epstein-Barr virus (EBV), have been linked to triggering Hashimoto's disease. To achieve remission, it is essential to identify and eliminate your personal triggers, which may include these pathogens. It's important to remember that not everyone with Hashimoto's has the same triggers; therefore, customizing your approach to treatment is crucial.

Epstein-Barr virus (EBV)

Epstein-Barr virus (EBV) is very common, having affected more than 90% of adults. Once infected, the virus usually remains in the body for life. Having evolved over millions of years, EBV has developed mechanisms to evade the immune system and persist. Studies indicate that EBV is associated with various autoimmune diseases, including systemic lupus, multiple sclerosis, rheumatoid arthritis, Sjögren's syndrome, and autoimmune hepatitis. The virus is also found in individuals with autoimmune thyroid disorders. While not the sole cause of these conditions, EBV may play a role in triggering or exacerbating autoimmune thyroid diseases.

H. pylori

Research indicates that *H. pylori*, a bacterium mainly spread through contaminated food or water, is well adapted to surviving in the stomach. Unlike many bacteria, *H. pylori* has evolved over about 60,000 years and is adept at evading our immune system, making it challenging for the body to effectively fight off the infection. While most individuals with *H. pylori* do not exhibit symptoms, those who do may experience sensations similar to indigestion. However, the infection can progressively damage the gastric mucosa over time, eventually impairing gastric function and leading to complications such as ulcers or gastric cancers. Additionally, *H. pylori* has been linked to both autoimmune and non-autoimmune thyroid disorders. Research suggests that treating and eradicating *H. pylori* can reduce levels of certain antibodies related to thyroid disorders, hinting at a potential connection between the bacteria and thyroid health.

Note: *There is both, a conventional and holistic approach that can be taken for* H. pylori *eradication. For me personally, I took a holistic approach with a trained Functional Medicine practitioner.*

Secretory IgA (SIgA)

Secretory IgA (SIgA) acts as the gut's initial shield, safeguarding it against toxins and harmful pathogens. It does this by blocking these invaders from getting through the gut lining and trapping them in mucus to be removed from our bodies. SIgA also helps to keep our gut healthy and balanced, which is important for our immune system. Recent research has shown that SIgA can directly stop certain harmful bacterial activities, influence the types of good bacteria in our gut, move antigens across the gut lining to specialized cells to help combat germs, and reduce the inflammation caused by pathogens and allergens. These studies also highlight SIgA's role in maintaining mucosal immunity and gut balance. Therefore, when levels are suppressed, from prolonged inflammation or infection, it points towards a compromised mucosal immune system leading to leaky gut, which can lead to even further dysbiosis. When levels are elevated it can be a sign of the immune system's activated defense, while this can be a protective reponse, persistently elevated levels can indicate underlying chronic inflammation and chronic diseases, exposure to food allergies/sensitivities, or environmental toxins that irritate the GI-tract.

Anti-gliadin IgA

Gliadin is a part of gluten, the protein in wheat and other grains like barley and rye. If there are anti-gliadin antibodies that show up on a stool test, it can indicate an immune reaction in the gut to gluten in the diet. Researchers found that gliadin can bind to a specific receptor in our body (CXCR3), which then can cause an increase in intestinal permeability (leaky gut), meaning that gliadin and other foreign substances can pass through the gut into the bloodstream. In people who are genetically more likely to have this reaction, gliadin can attract and activate certain types of immune cells, which can lead to inflammation in the intestines.

β-glucuronidase

Beta-glucuronidase is an enzyme that is produced and regulated by the bacteria in the digestive system. This enzyme reverses the glucuronidation step of detoxification in order to regulate the level of hormones in the body. Think of it as a feedback pathway that helps to maintain the balance of hormones that the body needs to function. Unfortunately, when the gastrointestinal system is out of balance, beta-glucuronidase levels rise. This rise then uncouples or reverses the glucuronidation step that is trying to eliminate harmful levels of toxins, hormones, and other substances from the body. Therefore, high levels can indicate overexposure to toxins, problems detoxing (expecially estrogen), and/or dysbiosis.

Leaky gut

The intestinal barrier is a critical component of gut health, composed of various elements such as a sticky mucous layer, epithelial cells, defense and immune cells, muscles, and nerves. When this barrier is compromised, it can lead to conditions like leaky gut, in which disruptions result in functional issues and disease. But does our body know how to fix this problem? Yes, normally it does! The intestinal epithelium continuously regenerates, producing new cells that move up to the surface and eventually shed off. To maintain the barrier's integrity, a sophisticated mechanism activates when cells stretch, signaling proteins to redistribute from the tight junctions around the cells to fill any gaps left by shedding cells. This process effectively keeps harmful substances out. However, during inflammation, such as from infections or other illnesses, the rate of cell shedding may increase. If this happens too quickly, protein redistribution might not fully compensate, leading to larger openings in the barrier that allow harmful substances to pass through.

If you still have no idea what any of that means, let me break it down in a more relatable way: Our gut lining contains small holes that normally allow only water and nutrients to pass into the bloodstream. However, these holes can become larger due to inflammation, illness, or infection. When they enlarge, unwanted substances from the gut can leak into the bloodstream. This leakage triggers our immune system to respond, as it perceives these substances as foreign invaders. The result is a cycle of increased inflammation throughout the body. It's also important to note that leaky gut can be influenced by other factors, such as stress, changes in the beneficial gut bacteria, alcohol consumption, a Western-style diet, and diseases that cause inflammation or ulcers.

Additional Tests

Outside of the GI-MAP™ and a full thyroid panel, additional tests can be run depending on the provider you are working with and what makes sense for your particular situation. Such tests include heavy metal testing, vitamin and mineral analysis, and a comprehensive metabolic panel, among many others. For my particular case, we did heavy metal testing.

Metals are naturally occurring elements, with some, like iron, zinc, magnesium, selenium, and copper, being essential in small amounts for human bodily functions. However, the excessive presence of metals such as lead, mercury, arsenic, and cadmium can result in toxicity, even at low levels of exposure. Symptoms of toxic metal exposure include fatigue, dehydration, nausea, and weakness. Exposure to heavy metals can happen through skin contact, inhalation, or ingestion via various sources like water, smoke, industrial or agricultural activities, paints, dental care, food contamination, and occupational exposure. This constant risk of exposure underscores the importance of testing for heavy metals as a crucial piece in solving a complex health puzzle.

Heavy metal: Cadmium found

Cadmium, a toxic metal, disrupts hormones because it acts as an endocrine disruptor. It is ubiquitous, found in everything from natural environments to pollution from factories and farms. People can become significantly exposed to cadmium through tobacco smoking and their diet. Studies show that even low environmental doses can disrupt thyroid function. Additionally, cadmium has been linked to autoimmune diseases and thyroid cancer. As an endocrine disruptor, cadmium alters normal pituitary secretion, making it difficult for the pituitary gland to secrete TSH.

Note: *When cadmium was found in a high amount, my Functional Medicine provider asked if I smoke/ed. I thought his question was odd at the time, but I shared with him that I did not smoke, but both my parents had since I was little. Remember when I said earlier that everything you are exposed to and experience impacts your health?*

Next, I want to share a few important results from the tests conducted by my primary care doctor, which are strongly linked to hypothyroidism:

Ferritin

Hypothyroidism is often linked to low levels of ferritin, a blood protein that stores iron. This deficiency can negatively impact the thyroid gland and its crucial functions. Iron is necessary for the thyroid peroxidase (TPO) enzyme, which helps create thyroid hormones by modifying thyroglobulin with iodine. Additionally, studies have shown that iron deficiency can reduce the conversion of T4 to T3 and interfere with the regulation of thyroid metabolism at the central level. Low levels can mean your body isn't absorbing iron from the diet properly or your body has an inadequate amount of red blood cells so symptoms like fatigue, dizziness, and a fast heartbeat can envelope you. High levels can indicate your body is storing too much iron or from conditions that cause inflammation.

Vitamin D

Vitamin D plays a role in maintaining calcium balance. The thyroid gland produces calcitonin, a hormone that helps to lower calcium levels in the blood. Conversely, parathyroid hormone stimulates an enzyme that converts vitamin D, which your skin produces when exposed to sunlight, into calcitriol (an active form of vitamin D). This process increases calcium levels. Studies have shown that low levels of vitamin D are associated with autoimmune hypothyroidism.

Note: *When my vitamin D came back low, it was two points above being in the 'red' and I was told I was 'fine'. I believe it is important to pay attention to these results. Being "fine" is not the same as being optimal.*

Vitamin B12

Studies show that patients with hypothyroidism have low levels of vitamin B12. Vitamin B12, or cobalamin, is involved in metabolism and used as a cofactor in DNA synthesis. It is hydrochloric acid (stomach acid) that removes B12 from food, so if you have low stomach acid, digestive diseases, or a rare condition in which your stomach does not produce an intrinsic factor, then B12 cannot be absorbed, leading to a deficiency. This underscores the significance of evaluating gut health, particularly in ensuring the effective absorption and utilization of essential vitamins and minerals by the body.

Note: *My vitamin B12 came back low but 'normal'*

Testing provides valuable information that can guide personalized interventions and monitor progress over time. It offers the insights necessary for experts to make adjustments to your treatment plan, leading to improved outcomes and better overall health. By conducting specific tests, healthcare providers can gather objective data about your health status, enabling a targeted approach to address any underlying issues. This targeted approach not only helps identify the root causes of symptoms but also ensures that the treatment plan is tailored to your unique needs. Ultimately, testing empowers both you and your provider to make informed decisions about your health, leading to more precise and effective treatment strategies. By relying on evidence-based testing rather than guessing, you can work toward achieving optimal wellness. This means focusing on optimal health rather than just meeting standard norms.

For me, testing was crucial; it confirmed that my symptoms were not imagined or merely anxiety-driven. Functional testing shed light on my situation and validated my concerns. Armed with this newfound knowledge from exploring my history, unraveling clues, and conducting Functional Medicine tests, it was time to unmask the underlying culprits and create a personalized treatment plan.

CHAPTER 5

Unmasking the Underlying Culprits

*"It is more important to understand the
imbalances in your body's basic systems and
restore balance, rather than name the disease and
match the pill to the ill." -Mark Hyman, M.D.*

*E*very day, our bodies strive to maintain balance,
but they face greater challenges in today's rapidly
evolving world. With an array of factors constantly
threatening to overwhelm our systems, it is essential to
uncover the underlying issues. Illness and disease often stem
from a combination of numerous triggers, yet we often find
ourselves surprised or puzzled when we fall ill, not realizing
the extent of our exposure to harmful substances. In an earlier
chapter, I discussed encountering various triggers in my
health journey, including *H. pylori*, Epstein-Barr virus, heavy
metal accumulation, and leaky gut. Additionally, I discovered
a gluten sensitivity and consistent exposure to fluoride and
toxic substances in household and personal care products.
Neglecting hydration and physical activity further hindered

my body's detoxification processes. By identifying the root causes, we can eliminate harmful elements and restore balance to the body. This process involves identifying and addressing triggers like pathogens, chemicals, heavy metals, and the quality of our food and water. In this chapter, we will briefly touch on the detox system, how it works, and how it can become overwhelmed, alongside some common triggers for Hashimoto's.

Detox System

In our world, toxins abound, from pollution and heavy metals to pesticides, processed foods, and a variety of harmful chemicals like neurotoxins and endocrine disruptors. Additionally, threats such as bacteria, viruses, parasites, and fungi can overwhelm our systems when they proliferate. So, how are we not sick all the time? Despite this onslaught, our bodies are equipped with their own detoxification systems, including the excretory organs such as the skin, lungs, large intestine, kidneys, and, notably, liver. Their roles in detoxification are as follows:

- **Skin**: Apart from regulating body temperature, sweating helps eliminate excess water, salts, and small amounts of urea.

- **Lungs**: The lungs inhale oxygen and exhale carbon dioxide and water vapor.

- **Large Intestine**: The large intestine absorbs remaining water and indigestible material and excretes it via stool.

- **Kidneys**: The kidneys eliminate excess water and waste from the bloodstream via urine.

- **Liver**: Blood coming from the digestive organs flows to the liver, carrying toxic substances (as well as nutrients and medication). Once they reach the liver, these substances are processed, stored, altered, detoxified, and passed back into the blood or released in the bowel to be eliminated. It is important to note that the liver detoxification process comprises two phases—phase one involves breaking down fat-soluble toxins, while phase two focuses on making these toxins water-soluble for removal.

In our bodies, the internal detox system operates tirelessly, but it can become overwhelmed by the volume of toxins it must process, especially if the liver itself suffers from dysfunction due to factors such as genetics, viral infections, or alcohol. Additionally, the system can be affected when processes upstream of the liver, such as digestion, are dysfunctional. In hypothyroidism, things tend to be slowed down and that can cause liver congestion and poor bile flow which would lead to retention and recirculation of toxins, along with, fatty acid and vitamin deficiencies. The type of toxin, its quantity, your frequency of exposure, and your overall health status all influence the likelihood of falling ill due to toxins.

Scenario: Think of your body's detoxification process like a shower drain. Initially, it efficiently drains the water, but as hair accumulates, it gradually clogs up. Ignored, the drain becomes increasingly obstructed until water backup occurs. Similarly, continually adding toxins without supporting the detoxification mechanisms can overwhelm the body's capacity, which can lead to symptoms—your body's way of telling you something is wrong.

For instance, when your skin becomes clogged, you may notice pimples or acne. If your lungs can't efficiently expel carbon dioxide (their waste product), you might experience headaches, shortness of breath, or sluggishness. When kidney function slows down, symptoms can include muscle cramps, sleep problems, dry and itchy skin, dark urine, and frequent urination. If your liver becomes congested, you may experience itchy skin, easy bruising, tremors, abdominal pain, weakness, and confusion. It is essential to heed these signals and address the root cause to restore balance and well-being.

Now that you have gained insight into the organs responsible for detoxification, their processes, and the signs of congestion, you can appreciate the significance of supporting these organs.

Toxic Burden

Endocrine disruptors

Knowing that chemicals like PCBs and BPA are structurally similar to T4, it is crucial to discuss some of the most well-known and extensively studied endocrine disruptors:

- **Atrazine:** Farmers all over the world use this popular herbicide to control weeds in corn, sugarcane, and sorghum farms. Studies have shown that frequent exposure to this chemical can cause harm to the kidneys, liver, and heart.

- **Bisphenol A (BPA):** BPA is an industrial chemical used in the production of polycarbonate plastics and epoxy resins. It is also used to manufacture food containers, leading to a high risk of it leaching into canned foods and beverages from the inner surfaces of these containers. BPA is harmful to both the brain and the prostate gland.

- **Dioxins:** Dioxins are also called persistent chemical pollutants. They occur as a byproduct of manufacturing processes like paper bleaching and herbicide production. They're highly toxic to the endocrine system, the immune system, and even the reproductive system.

- **Perchlorate:** Perchlorate is also dangerous to thyroid health, as it disrupts the production of thyroid hormones by reducing iodine uptake. This colorless salt is used industrially in rocket production, but human exposure to large doses can result in severe thyroid malfunction.

- **Per- and polyfluoroalkyl substances (PFAS):** These groups of chemicals are used to make heat-, water-, grease-, and oil-resistant coatings for nonstick pans. Human exposure to them can impair thyroid function and compromise immune health.

- **Phthalates:** Phthalates are used to make durable plastics and dissolve other chemical materials. They're also used in making products like cosmetics, vinyl flooring, and lubricating oils. Exposure to large amounts of phthalates can cause hormonal imbalance and disrupt the endocrine system.

○ Research indicates that a large percentage of the population, approximately 99%, is regularly exposed to fragrance products. These products contain a complex mixture of chemicals, with various sources contributing to this exposure. For instance, 84.1% of people encounter fragrances from laundry products, 79.9% from cleaning products, 77% from household items, and 72.2% from air fresheners. Alarmingly, 34.7% of individuals have reported experiencing negative health effects due to fragrance exposure, with respiratory issues being the most common complaint.

In the United States, laws are in place to safeguard public health and the environment. However, these regulations do not require full disclosure of all ingredients in products that contain fragrances. When a product label lists only "fragrance," consumers remain unaware of the specific chemicals present in the product. This lack of transparency also applies to other items such as air fresheners, laundry supplies, and cleaning products, which are not required to disclose their full ingredient list. Although personal care products and cosmetics must list their ingredients, the individual chemicals in the fragrance blend are not disclosed, leaving consumers uninformed.

○ Scented candles, especially paraffin wax candles, should be avoided, as they are toxic due to either carcinogenic compounds created when lit or lead wiring in the wicks.

- **Phytoestrogens:** Phytoestrogens are structurally similar to β-estradiol. They occur naturally in plants like soy foods. They can exhibit hormone-like activities, thereby disrupting actual hormones from performing their functions.

- **Polybrominated diphenyl ethers (PBDEs):** PBDEs are industrial chemicals used in the manufacture of fire extinguishers, plastics, and furniture foam. They can also disrupt the endocrine system.

- **Polychlorinated biphenyls (PCBs):** PCBs are highly carcinogenic chemicals. Before their ban, these chemicals were used in the production of lubricants, plasticizers, hydraulic fluids, transformers, and other electrical equipment.

- **Triclosan:** Triclosan, an antimicrobial agent used in soaps, detergents, and personal care products, can also disrupt the endocrine system.

Taking a look at what you are potentially exposing yourself to daily is a good starting point. Consider this: The average woman encounters 168 chemicals a day just from common products. When you factor in environmental pollutants from household products, cookware, air, water, and food (more than 10,000 chemicals are allowed in food sold in the US), your toxic load can significantly increase. Once you are aware of the potential exposure, you can then make an informed decision on whether to continue to use them or seek alternatives.

Heavy Metals

Mercury

There are three forms of mercury: elemental, inorganic, and organic. Mercury exposure can occur through consuming contaminated fish or inhaling vapor from volcanoes, forest fires, or human activities, including burning coal and fossil fuels, mining mercury, and refining precious metals. Additionally, the manufacture of electrical and automotive parts, chemical releases through incineration, landfills, and industrial contamination of water systems can also expose individuals to large amounts of mercury. Elemental mercury can accumulate in our central nervous system and kidneys, while inorganic mercury tends to accumulate in the kidneys and liver after absorption.

Cadmium and lead

The general population is exposed to cadmium and lead through various sources, such as ambient air, drinking water, food, industrial materials, and consumer products.

- Cadmium exposure has been linked to changes in the levels of thyroid hormone and the precursor hormone TG. Additionally, its toxicity is connected to dysfunction in the lungs, kidneys, liver, bones, reproductive system, and cardiovascular system. Classified as a Group 1 human carcinogen, this non-essential metal can be encountered through inhalation (emissions from industrial activities, including mining, smelting, and manufacturing of batteries, pigments, stabilizers, and alloys), cigarette smoke, or contaminated food.

- Lead exposure is known to cause neurological and hematological issues, as well as damage to the kidneys, liver, and reproductive system in humans.

As I examined my surroundings, it became clear that a significant overhaul was necessary. Plastic storage containers, deteriorating cookware, air fresheners, candles, old mattresses and linens, cleaning products, and personal care products—all needed replacing. However, this transformation was not an overnight process; it took years of gradual transitions. A key lesson I quickly learned was the ironic reality that health-conscious products often come with a higher price tag. It seems counterintuitive, doesn't it? The affordable options are usually detrimental to health, while the beneficial ones are costly. Considering this, I advise against overwhelming yourself mentally or financially by trying to swap out everything all at once. However, if that approach suits you and doesn't present a burden, go for it!

Following the detoxification of my living space, my focus shifted toward improving the quality of my food and water.

Food and Water Toxins

Our body performs important functions such as breaking down food, absorbing nutrients, and protecting us from illness. These activities also help keep our immune system functioning properly. The foods we eat, including carbohydrates, proteins, and fats, can influence the different types of bacteria living in our bodies. These bacteria produce chemicals called metabolites, which can have either beneficial or detrimental effects on the gut and immune system.

For example, the typical Western-style diet, which includes lots of red meat, butter, processed grains, sugary foods, and fewer fruits and veggies, can be harmful to our gut health. This is because the ingredients in modern processed foods can harm the gut lining and change the balance of bacteria in our gut, leading to problems like obesity and gut inflammation. Let's take a closer look:

- Simple sugars and emulsifiers can harm the lining of our gut by encouraging the growth of harmful bacteria that break down the protective mucous layer.

- Alcohol, high-glucose foods, and high-fructose foods trigger gut inflammation and damage the gut lining, leading to a "leaky gut"—which can allow harmful pathogens to move into our bloodstream, causing infection and inflammation.

- Processed foods commonly contain additives such as MSG, sodium nitrates, sulfites, trans fats, and FD&C Yellow 5 and 6, as well as artificial sweeteners like Ace K and aspartame. Although these additives may seem safe, recent studies suggest that they contribute to health issues such as metabolic syndrome and inflammation by negatively affecting the gut microbiome.

- Cyanotoxins are harmful substances found in water and seafood—including fish, mussels, and crustaceans—contaminated by cyanobacteria. These toxins have been linked to triggering gut inflammation and harming the cells lining the gut, thereby increasing the permeability of the intestinal wall, often described as "leaky gut." Moreover, cyanotoxins can indirectly influence the levels of thyroid hormones T3 and T4, either through inflammatory gut reactions or imbalances in gut bacteria. They may also directly impact the thyroid gland itself.

- Pro-inflammatory foods can lead to autoimmune diseases and metabolic syndrome. These foods include processed meats, grilled and smoked meats, alcohol (how many husbands are upset right now?), refined carbohydrates (these are your cakes, cookies, white bread, pasta, and sugary drinks), hydrogenated vegetable oils, margarine, sucrose/fructose/glucose/high-fructose corn syrup, and gluten.

- High fluoride concentrations in water have been linked with higher TSH values.

- Drinking water contaminated with heavy metals, such as arsenic, cadmium, mercury, and lead, poses significant health risks. When the levels of these non-biodegradable metals exceed permissible limits, they can cause severe toxicity. Furthermore, because these metals accumulate in the ecosystem, they pose ongoing risks to human health. Additionally, water packaging materials have recently become notable sources of heavy metal contamination in bottled water.

In an effort to calm my inflamed and overactive immune system, I embarked on an elimination diet. Before this, my eating habits mirrored those of many Americans, following a typical Western diet without paying much attention to labels or the impact of my food choices. I did not consider how certain foods affected my body or monitor my intake of macronutrients. I also neglected proper hydration, only drinking one to two bottles of water daily, and often skipped meals or opted for quick, low-calorie microwave meals without much consideration for nutritional value (this is the part where all the nutritionists and dieticians cringe).

Upon starting the elimination diet—which is not a lifelong diet but is only meant for a period of 30–90 days—I cut out inflammatory food groups such as dairy, gluten, soy, sugar, caffeine, alcohol, grains, and condiments. You might be wondering, *What the hell is there left to eat?*

The answer: Whole foods, returning to basics, and focusing on nourishing the body. This means focusing on shopping the perimeter of the store, where everything has *one ingredient:* apples, oranges, kiwi, papaya, blueberries, kale, bok choy, spinach, squash, etc.

After receiving guidance from my Functional Medicine practitioner, I embarked on the elimination diet for two months before adding foods back in slowly. I won't sugarcoat it—the initial week was tough. I was constantly hungry as I navigated this new way of eating. It quickly became clear that this wasn't a diet to tackle without preparation. By the end of that first week, I learned that success depended heavily on proper food preparation. Having meals and snacks ready significantly eased my hunger pangs and prevented moments of weakness. Another challenge was watching others enjoy foods I couldn't have. Thankfully, the support from my husband, who joined me on this journey, made meal prepping and adherence to the diet much more manageable.

Note: *Remember when I mentioned how important having support is for your health?*

I adhered to the elimination diet for 60 days before gradually reintroducing food groups, one at a time, each week. This slow process helped me identify specific foods that triggered symptoms like headaches, rashes, and digestive issues. Food sensitivities differ from allergies as their symptoms can appear up to 72 hours later, making it crucial to maintain a food journal during this phase. Ultimately, I pinpointed the foods that caused my most severe symptoms, with gluten being the primary culprit. I then avoided gluten for an additional two months before attempting to reintroduce it. However, gluten continued to cause problems, leading me to eliminate it permanently from my diet. While this strict avoidance isn't necessary for everyone with Hashimoto's, experts note that many with the condition are particularly sensitive to gluten, soy, and dairy.

The key term I want you to focus on here is "trying again." You see, food sensitivity testing and elimination diets often spark debate and scrutiny. Having undergone both myself, I have come to understand the controversies surrounding them. Food sensitivity testing, while informative, offers a *snapshot in time* that potentially presents a long list of foods to avoid. Many individuals may end up eliminating these foods indefinitely, leading to a very restrictive diet devoid of essential nutrients. Similarly, the elimination diet can result in individuals steering clear of certain foods forever if they find them intolerable. It is crucial to grasp that these findings are not necessarily permanent directives, unless there is a genuine allergy involved. In reality, these sensitivities likely stem from frequent consumption coupled with the probable presence of a leaky gut. As you already learned, certain foods or diets, like the Western-style diet, have negative effects on the intestinal barrier. The compromised gut barrier allows undigested food particles into the bloodstream, triggering inflammation and immune reactions.

Identifying trigger foods is crucial for their temporary elimination during the healing process. Ideally, once the gut is restored to its optimal state, these foods should no longer pose a threat. However, it is important to remain mindful of the foods and heavily processed diets that can contribute to the breakdown of the gut barrier. After all, there is little point in healing and sealing your gut if you revert to consuming the same inflammatory toxins that will damage it again. Furthermore, our individuality significantly influences our tolerance levels; what may cause issues for one person might be well tolerated by another. For example, while some may indulge in gluten occasionally without any repercussions, others may need to avoid it entirely. Recognizing and respecting these unique dietary needs and responses is essential for achieving optimal health and well-being.

Note: *Weight loss was never, ever the goal for us, but surprisingly, I managed to shed ten pounds and my husband lost a remarkable 30 pounds on the same diet. His commitment to supporting me also improved his own health, and I couldn't be more proud of him. Interestingly enough, a study of 100 women with Hashimoto's showed an elimination diet was a more effective tool in reducing body fat mass in women with Hashimoto's disease than standard balanced reducing diets with the same energy value and main nutrient content. It also showed lower antibodies and TSH as well!*

Individualized Protocol

Working alongside a Functional Medicine practitioner, I followed a customized protocol to eliminate heavy metals, chemicals, viruses, and excess bacteria from my body through supplements, food, and lifestyle changes. While supplements can be beneficial, it is important to have a clear rationale for their use rather than blindly following trends or using them as temporary fixes.

Note: *I highly recommend working with a Functional Medicine practitioner that aligns with you to develop a protocol tailored specifically to your bodies needs.*

In summary, we talked about how 70% of the immune system is in the gut, and we talked about leaky gut (intestinal permeability) and the factors that create it. Now, in addition to identifying leaky gut and the causes of it, we need to fix it, right? This is necessary to ensure that those foreign substances do not continue to leak into the bloodstream and keep causing systemic inflammation and immune reactions. We need to seal up those tight junctions, and part of that involves bringing down any inflammation (e.g., from foods). That is why we talked about an elimination diet, which removes inflammatory foods. Then, reducing inflammation from pathogens (bacteria, viruses, fungi, yeast, and parasites) is where the eradication protocol came into play. Now it is time to talk about what things can help heal and support thyroid and gut health!

CHAPTER 6

Nourishing from Within: The Power of Food

"Each of the substances of a man's diet acts upon his body and changes it in some way and upon these changes his whole life depends." -Hippocrates

During my treatment within the conventional healthcare system, the emphasis was primarily on prescribing medications, with little to no guidance on nutrition and lifestyle. As a result, I lacked the necessary education and resources to support my thyroid and immune health through daily practices. I was left to navigate my health journey alone. Thankfully, by incorporating a Functional Medicine practitioner into my healthcare team, I have filled this gap, and now I have the opportunity to enlighten you!

Everything is connected. Our body operates as *one* system, not separate parts. So as we dive into this chapter on healing through food, I will be talking about different parts of the body that need some extra love and support from you when it comes to healing your thyroid.

Gut Health

As you are now aware, the food we consume can disrupt the delicate balance of our gut ecosystem. This is why maintaining a nutritionally balanced diet is essential for supporting a healthy gut microbiome, nurturing the integrity of the gut lining, and fostering immune tolerance.

- The intestinal lining consists of a single layer of epithelial cells connected by tight junction proteins. These cells, such as absorptive enterocytes and Paneth cells, play vital roles in nutrient absorption and combating harmful bacteria.

- Goblet cells secrete mucus that serves as a protective barrier over the epithelium. If this mucus barrier is compromised, bacteria and undigested food can reach the epithelial cells and cause inflammation. In a healthy gut, there is a balance between beneficial bacteria and the mucous layer.

- The beneficial bacteria residing in our gut, known as commensal bacteria, play a crucial role in maintaining the integrity of the epithelial barrier. These bacteria produce energy in the form of short-chain fatty acids and release substances that combat harmful bacteria. Additionally, short-chain fatty acids can directly strengthen the tight junctions, further enhancing the integrity of our gut barrier.

- Dietary-fiber-derived short-chain fatty acids promote the health of our intestinal lining. They do so by increasing the production of mucus and releasing a substance called Il-18, which can help in repairing the epithelium. When our diet lacks dietary fiber, certain types of bacteria that feed on mucus increase in number, causing the mucus layer to become thin.

Gut-supporting foods include vitamins A and D, probiotics, short-chain fatty acids, fiber, polyphenols (quercetin), glutamine, and fermented foods. Let's take a closer look.

Short-chain fatty acids = butyrate, propionate, and acetate

Short-chain fatty acids are produced by the gut during the fermentation of polycarbohydrates. There are three main types: butyrate, propionate, and acetate. The butyrate-producing bacteria in the gut are particularly important because they actively influence and control the balance of microorganisms. They achieve this by producing antimicrobial and anti-inflammatory molecules that help maintain a healthy gut environment. These bacteria regulate immune responses and protect against pathogens without causing inflammation or hyper-responsiveness by shaping the gut's microbial community. Additionally, butyrate is utilized by gut cells for energy, enhancing oxygen availability and maintaining an anaerobic environment that discourages harmful bacteria, such as *Salmonella* and *E. coli*, from colonizing. It is also significant to note that these microbial communities, especially those that produce butyrate, can inhibit the growth of cancer cells by releasing substances with anti-cancer properties. Indigestible dietary fibers are commonly used as prebiotics; however, polyphenols can also function as prebiotics, significantly increasing the abundance of butyrate producers.

Fiber

In Western countries, fiber intake is well below recommended levels. This is a problem because, as was just stated above, low-fiber diets promote the growth of mucus-degrading bacteria, which eats away at our intestinal lining. Dietary fiber is the key to maintaining diverse and healthy gut microbiota, as well as, aiding in our bodies ability to rid toxins and excess hormones.

Fiber-rich foods- lentils, split peas, black beans, pinto beans, artichoke hearts, kidney beans, chickpeas, chia seeds, blackberries, raspberries, pears, almonds, oats, broccoli, quinoa, Hass avocados, apples, green peas, edamame, brussels sprouts, and ground flaxseed

Fermented Foods

During the fermentation process, microorganisms convert food into products that are more nutritious and have additional functional properties, like probiotics, which are beneficial bacteria for our gut health; prebiotics, which provide the foods for the good bacteria in our gut; and biogenics, which are substances that have a positive effect on our biological functions.

Fermented foods- kefir, kombucha, sauerkraut, miso, and yogurt.

Immune System

The main hub of our immune system is situated just beneath the layer of epithelial cells lining our intestinal wall. These immune cells are crucial for fending off infections and maintaining the protective barrier of the intestinal mucosa. The interplay between the beneficial bacteria (commensals) and the immune system is dynamic and mutually influential, with both parties impacting each other. The composition and diversity of gut bacteria can be influenced by our diet, as various nutrients serve as substrates for bacterial growth. Additionally, certain nutrients can directly influence immune cells, affecting their activity and function.

Vitamin A

Vitamin A plays a vital role in maintaining the structural and functional integrity of epithelial tissues in various parts of the body, so a deficiency can impact the skin, eyes, sweat glands, salivary glands, and respiratory tract. According to research, vitamin A deficiency is closely linked to both structural and functional problems in the thyroid gland and is frequently found alongside iodine deficiency. As a fat-soluble vitamin, it can be readily stored in the body, especially in liver and fat tissue. It exists in two forms: an active form, called retinol; and a precursor that needs to be converted into vitamin A, known as carotenoids. Since the human body cannot produce vitamin A on its own, it must be obtained through dietary sources. Zinc and fatty meals can enhance the absorption of vitamin A. It is important to consume vitamin A in moderate amounts, as excessive consumption can lead to toxicity, with the vitamin easily accumulating in liver and fat tissue.

- Carotenoid foods (the ripest fruit holds the most carotenoids)- pumpkin, carrot, sweet potato, winter squash, cantaloupe, red pepper, tomato, kale, spinach, broccoli, mango, grapefruit, papaya, guava, dates, rose hip, dill, and basil

- Retinol foods- milk (the higher the fat content, the more retinol), eggs, cod liver oil, liver of various livestock, and fish

Vitamin C

As humans, we are unable to synthesize vitamin C and must, therefore, obtain it from our diet. Vitamin C, also known as L-ascorbic acid, is an essential nutrient that acts as a vital cofactor for numerous enzymes involved in various processes, such as the proper formation of connective tissue and hormone synthesis. There is some evidence in current research that shows vitamin C could improve free T4, T3, and TSH concentration. It also enhances the absorption of iron. While vitamin C is generally non-toxic, it is important to note that high doses have been known to cause rare but documented cases of kidney stones.

Vitamin C foods- star fruit, guava, black currant, kiwi, strawberry, camu camu, acerola cherry, broccoli, kale, peppers, sauerkraut, and citrus fruit

Vitamin D

Vitamin D is a fat-soluble vitamin essential for the body, with its receptors playing a crucial role in regulating gut microbiota and immune responses. This vitamin strengthens the body's barrier function by enhancing the expression of tight junction proteins and also supports bone health and immune function. It has also shown promise in reducing thyroid antibody levels, enhancing thyroid function, and improving other indicators of autoimmunity, according to research. Diet contributes only 10–20% of our vitamin D intake, while about 90% is synthesized in the skin through exposure to UVB light. Because of this, insufficient sun exposure is a common cause of vitamin D deficiency—a reminder to get outside or perhaps book that vacation.

Vitamin D receptors belong to a group of proteins that includes receptors for steroid hormones, thyroid hormones, and vitamin A metabolites, as well as various cholesterol metabolites, bile acids, and fatty acids. Vitamin D metabolism relies on magnesium as a cofactor; therefore, a magnesium deficiency can hinder the transport and activation of vitamin D. Magnesium also plays a critical role in synthesizing and releasing parathyroid hormones, which become suppressed in states of magnesium depletion. Insufficient dietary magnesium intake can affect the response of the parathyroid gland to vitamin D, exacerbating deficiencies in both. The interplay between magnesium and vitamin D can create a detrimental cycle, potentially worsening these deficits. Additionally, vitamin D promotes the absorption of calcium and phosphate in the intestines, the reabsorption of calcium in the renal tubules, and the mobilization of calcium from the bones.

Vitamin D foods- cod liver oil, rainbow trout, salmon, canned sardines, canned tuna, and raw mushrooms exposed to UV light

Selenium

Selenium is notably found in the highest concentration in the thyroid gland. Selenium plays a crucial role in antioxidant functions and the metabolism of thyroid hormones. Research has highlighted a link between selenium deficiency and autoimmune thyroid conditions, concluding that selenium supplementation could significantly reduce thyroid autoantibodies in patients with Hashimoto's disease and also impair the conversion of T4 to T3. This micronutrient also has significant immune stimulatory effects.

Note: *Interestingly, in a clinical trial conducted in Italy in 2017, 168 patients with Hashimoto's were given a combination of myo-inositol and selenium supplementation for six months. The results showed significant improvements in symptoms and thyroid function parameters. The study concluded that 83 mcg of selenium supplementation with 600 mg of inositol daily significantly improved their symptoms and restored the euthyroid state.*

Selenium foods- Brazil nuts, yellowfin tuna, canned sardines, roasted ham, boneless roasted turkey, pan-fried beef liver, roasted chicken, cottage cheese, brown rice, and hard-boiled eggs

Iron

Iron is an essential mineral critical for blood cell production and needed for the production of some hormones. Approximately 70% of the body's iron is in hemoglobin, a protein in red blood cells responsible for transporting oxygen. Iron also plays a vital role in immune health! Just as iron impacts the immune system, immune responses can alter iron metabolism. Iron deficiency is closely linked to hypothyroidism, and maintaining adequate iron levels is crucial for proper thyroid function. Also, gastric acid plays a role in the absorption of iron in the body; however, when gastric acid production is impaired—such as by acid-reducing medication—the absorption of iron is significantly reduced. This underscores the importance of examining gut health. Even with the cleanest diet, nutrient absorption can be compromised if there is underlying gut dysfunction.

Heme iron foods- beef, chicken, turkey, lamb, ham, pork, liver, veal, clams, and oysters

Non-heme iron foods- lentils, peas, tofu, soybeans, kidney beans, and garbanzo beans

Zinc

The essential role of zinc in the human body cannot be overstated. It acts as a potent antioxidant, anti-inflammatory agent, and immune regulator. It is also essential for thyroid hormone function! A zinc deficiency can increase susceptibility to autoimmune conditions and affect the gastrointestinal, central nervous, immune, skeletal, epidermal, and reproductive systems. About 70% of the zinc in circulation is bound to albumin, and any factor that alters serum albumin concentration can also impact serum zinc levels. Phytic acid, commonly found in all edible seeds, legumes, and nuts, significantly inhibits zinc absorption. However, its effects are confined to a single meal and do not impair zinc absorption throughout the entire day (unless such foods are consumed at every meal). Generally, protein intake enhances zinc absorption.

Zinc foods- oysters, beef sirloin, blue crab, pork chops, turkey breast, and cheddar cheese

Protein

Amino acids are the fundamental building blocks of proteins in our cells and tissues, underscoring their critical role in cell survival, maintenance, and proliferation. In humans, protein malnutrition has long been associated with immune defects and intestinal inflammation. The essential amino acid tryptophan is a key regulator of gut immunity. Glutamine, another essential amino acid, is the most abundant and versatile amino acid in the body, playing a vital role both in health and disease. While glucose is a crucial metabolite and the primary source of energy for many cells, immune system cells such as lymphocytes, neutrophils, and macrophages have a high demand for glutamine. The utilization of glutamine by these immune cells can rival or even surpass that of glucose. This high demand by immune cells and other tissues, like the liver, may exceed the available supply, potentially leading to glutamine deficiency. The survival, proliferation, and function of immune cells crucially depend on adequate glutamine levels to mount an effective defense against pathogens.

Protein foods- eggs, chicken, cottage cheese, greek yogurt, lentils, salmon, quinoa, spinach, cauliflower

Polyphenols

Polyphenols are divided into the following categories: phenolic acids, flavonoids, stilbenes, and lignans. They are antioxidants and exhibit anti-inflammatory activities. They have been shown to enhance antitumor immune activity, immunomodulatory processes, and intestinal mucosal immunity.

Polyphenol-rich foods (the darker the fruit, the greater the polyphenol content; also, local and in-season foods contain the highest nutritional value)- apples, pomegranates, berries, broccoli, carrots, dark chocolate, flax seed, ginger, green tea, spinach, olives, and olive oil.

Thyroid

The composition of the gut microbiota plays a significant role in determining the availability of essential micronutrients crucial for thyroid health. Iodine, iron, and copper are essential for synthesizing thyroid hormones; selenium and zinc are necessary for converting T4 to T3; and vitamin D helps regulate the immune response. For optimal thyroid function, regular consumption of vitamins A, B, C, and D, as well as magnesium, zinc, iron, and selenium, is paramount. Most of these micronutrients, as mentioned, also benefit the immune system and the gut, which is why they are listed above. Let's discuss the remaining ones.

B vitamins

There are eight essential B vitamins, all of which are water-soluble and require daily replenishment since the body does not store them. Serving as coenzymes, B vitamins play a crucial role in various enzymatic processes that support cellular functions, particularly within the brain and nervous system. A deficiency in B vitamins can disrupt mitochondrial metabolism, impacting the breakdown of amino acids, glucose, and fatty acids.

Vitamin B1

Vitamin B1, also known as thiamine, is absorbed in the duodenum. It requires magnesium as its cofactor, which helps in converting it into its active form, TPP. Insufficient levels of thiamine can lead to disrupted mitochondrial function, impaired oxidative metabolism, and decreased energy production, potentially resulting in cell death, particularly in high-energy-demanding neurons.

Foods enriched with B1 include whole grains, pork, fish, and yeast (especially when added to cereals).

Vitamin B2

Vitamin B2 is also known as riboflavin. Its active forms are essential for synthesizing niacin, folic acid, vitamin B6, and all heme proteins. It is indispensable for the metabolism of carbohydrates, proteins, and fats into glucose, and it plays a significant role in cellular respiration and immune system function due to its antioxidant properties.

Foods rich in B2 include eggs, dairy products, green vegetables, meat, mushrooms, and almonds. You can add these to rice, corn, and flour.

Vitamin B3

Vitamin B3 is also known as niacin. It is metabolized from tryptophan and serves as a precursor for coenzymes that are essential for DNA repair and cholesterol synthesis. Hence, this vitamin plays a critical role in overall cellular health and function.

B3-rich foods include plant-based foods like soy, nuts, seeds, legumes, and grains.

Vitamin B5

Also known as pantothenic acid, vitamin B5 is indispensable for the biosynthesis of coenzyme A, cholesterol, fatty acids, and acetylcholine. The role B5 plays in these processes underscores its importance in maintaining metabolic and neurological functions within the body.

You can get B5 in foods like fortified cereals, dried foods, mushrooms, eggs, fish, avocados, chicken, beef, pork, sunflower seeds, sweet potatoes, and lentils.

Vitamin B6

Also known as pyridoxine (or its active form, pyridoxal 5'-phosphate), vitamin B6 is a coenzyme that facilitates the function of numerous enzymes responsible for a wide range of functions. These functions include supporting the immune system, maintaining brain health, regulating homocysteine levels, and aiding in the breakdown of carbohydrates, proteins, and fats.

Foods rich in B6 include beef, poultry, starchy vegetables, noncitrus fruits, and fortified cereals.

Vitamin B7

Vitamin B7 is also known as biotin. It is involved in gene regulation, cell signaling, and replication. It catalyzes the metabolism of fatty acids, glucose, and amino acids, playing a critical role in energy production and cellular functions. It is important to note that high doses of biotin can potentially interfere with and affect the accuracy of tests for troponin, thyroid function, and vitamin D.

B7 occurs naturally in foods such as organ meats, eggs, fish, seeds, soybeans, and nuts.

Vitamin B9

Vitamin B9, also known as folate, is crucial for nucleic acid synthesis and red blood cell production.

Sources of B9 include foods such as dark green leafy vegetables, nuts, beans, dairy products, meat, poultry, grains, and Brussels sprouts.

It's important to note that people cannot synthesize folate. Naturally occurring folates, like those found in food, are susceptible to oxidation and are largely destroyed during cooking, which is why folic acid is often used as a supplement. However, folic acid does not occur naturally and has no biological function by itself. To be utilized from supplementation, the human body must metabolize and reduce it to 5-MTHF through a multistep enzymatic conversion. However, individuals with an MTHFR gene mutation—a condition that, according to the CDC, is very common—cannot process folate effectively. Therefore, experts often recommend supplementation with active folate, 5-MTHF, which bypasses the entire metabolization process of folate and is directly absorbed to exert its biological function.

Vitamin B12

Vitamin B12, also known as cobalamin, is essential for red blood cell production, neurological function, and myelin synthesis. It also acts as a cofactor in DNA and RNA synthesis, as well as in the metabolism of proteins, lipids, and hormones. Gut function comes into play here as gastric acid helps to release B12 from animal proteins to make it available for absorption. B12 is also a cofactor needed for methylation.

Magnesium

Magnesium is the fourth most abundant mineral in the human body and serves as a vital cofactor for over 300 enzymes. Its essential role supports various functions, including protein synthesis, neuromuscular coordination, cardiac function, and energy metabolism. Magnesium is also closely linked to the immune system, playing a significant role in managing oxidative stress and inflammation. It is also essential to supporting thyroid hormone production. It is primarily ingested through the diet, and the gastrointestinal system and kidneys work diligently to regulate its absorption and elimination, ensuring the body maintains optimal levels.

Magnesium foods- nuts, seeds, whole grains, dark chocolate, leafy greens, and fruits like papaya and bananas.

Iodine

Iodine is essential for thyroid hormone synthesis. However, both excessive and insufficient amounts can lead to hypothyroidism. Iodine, a trace element, is found in soil and water. In many countries, iodoprophylaxis programs have been implemented, which often involve the inclusion of iodized salt in households and the food industry. The iodine content in vegetables and fruits is heavily influenced by the soil, irrigation, and fertilizers used to grow them. For example, in China, the iodine concentration in water can be relatively high, leading to adequate or even excessive iodine intake. Conversely, in countries like Israel, where desalinated water is common, iodine levels are often very low. The highest iodine content is typically found in fish and marine plants.

Liver Detox Pathway Food Support

Given the potentially powerful impact of nutrients from food on detoxification pathways, the average individual should opt for a diet rich in a variety of whole foods.

Such foods include cruciferous veggies (cauliflower, broccoli, collard greens, radish, watercress, kale, Brussels sprouts, cabbage), berries (raspberries, blackberries, strawberries), soy, garlic, ginger, rosemary, turmeric, purple sweet potato, pomegranate, and ghee.

Heavy metals detox support

Numerous studies have highlighted the importance of essential metals, such as zinc, calcium, and iron, in preventing the absorption and toxicity of heavy metals like cadmium and lead. They do so by competing for absorption sites in the intestines and preventing tissue damage through competitive binding at enzyme sites.

- Zinc in particular has been extensively researched for its role in mitigating heavy metal toxicity. Due to its properties, which are similar to cadmium and lead, zinc competes with these toxic metals for metal absorptive and enzymatic process binding sites. The intake of zinc also triggers the production of a protein that binds tightly to cadmium, leading to its detoxification.

- Selenium, another essential element, has been found to protect against cadmium and lead toxicity in various parts of the body, including the brain, lungs, liver, kidneys, and blood. Selenium is a cofactor of the antioxidant enzyme glutathione peroxidase (GPx), and it contributes to the antioxidant defense system, which enables it to alleviate cadmium and lead toxicity. Additionally, selenium may form complexes with heavy metals, further aiding in their detoxification.

In essence, these essential metals play a crucial role in decreasing the absorption of cadmium and lead, restoring metal balance in the body, and combating the oxidative stress associated with heavy metal toxicity. Research recommends that people at risk of exposure to toxic metals should ensure a sufficient intake of essential elements and vitamins by increasing their consumption of vegetables and fruit. Some edible plants are particularly important as natural antagonists to cadmium and lead toxicity and should be consumed regularly. These include tomatoes, which are rich in iron, calcium, selenium, zinc, vitamins B and C, quercetin, and naringenin; berries, which are abundant in essential elements, vitamin C, anthocyanin, and catechin; onions, which are high in selenium, quercetin, and vitamins B and C; garlic, which contains sulfur-containing compounds, essential elements, and vitamins C and E; and grapes, which are rich in vitamins, essential elements, and anthocyanin.

So what is the perfect diet for Hashimoto's hypothyroidism?

Remember how we emphasized the uniqueness of every individual's body? In the same vein, every diet must also be unique. There isn't a one-size-fits-all diet for Hashimoto's hypothyroidism. While a gluten-free diet may be effective for some, it isn't necessarily the solution for everyone with Hashimoto's. The key to maintaining a nutritious diet is including foods that help reduce inflammation and support gut, immune, and thyroid health. This means avoiding inflammatory and heavily processed foods, chemicals, and toxins commonly found in the Western-style diet.

Anti-inflammatory lifestyle

Inflammation is often triggered by infections, trauma, toxins, or allergic reactions. If inflammation persists, it can lead to the development of various diseases, including autoimmune conditions. By incorporating anti-inflammatory elements into our diet, we can potentially reduce inflammation caused by illness and unhealthy eating habits. This underscores the dual role of diet in nourishing our bodies and as a form of medicine.

Gluten-free lifestyle

It is particularly recommended for those with Hahsimoto's because gluten is a major food sensitivity and contributor to leaky gut. Celiac disease, for example, and autoimmune thyroid disease share many genetic factors, almost as if they are siblings with common genes. Research suggests that the primary connection between consuming gluten and thyroid damage involves a process in which the body's immune system mistakenly targets thyroid tissue after being triggered by gluten in the gut. This resembles a case of mistaken identity between gut and thyroid tissues, leading to harm to the thyroid—a phenomenon known as molecular mimicry. Non-celiac gluten sensitivity, in where you have a celiac-like reaction but you don't test positive for celiac disease and is also associated with Hashimoto's! Not everyone *needs* to adopt a gluten-free diet; it is vital to understand how gluten *affects you personally.* In addition, it is important to note that gluten-free doesn't automatically mean it's 'healthy and clean' food. Many gluten-free products are still loaded with additives, fillers, gums, sugars, etc, so make sure you continue to read your labels!

Mediterranean lifestyle

Our diet can significantly impact our risk of autoimmune diseases. Consuming a diet high in unhealthy foods—that is, foods rich in animal fats and proteins, salt, and refined sugars (typical of the Western diet)—can disrupt the balance of our immune system and gut bacteria. This ultimately increases the likelihood of developing autoimmune conditions and causes inflammation and oxidative stress in the body. In contrast, the Mediterranean diet, renowned for its nutritional benefits, can positively influence our immune system, gut health, and overall body balance. Packed with antioxidants, anti-inflammatory substances, and immune-regulating properties, this diet acts as a shield against autoimmune diseases.

Recent studies have underscored the advantages of comprehensive dietary patterns like the Mediterranean diet in supporting our immune system and reducing inflammation. They have also shown that embracing a predominantly plant-based version of the Mediterranean diet may help to safeguard against thyroid autoimmunity. By cutting back on animal protein and incorporating more veggies and plant-based foods into our meals, we can potentially lower our risk of developing thyroid autoimmune disorders.

Paleo lifestyle

This type of diet emphasizes consuming local, sustainable, organic, and non-GMO foods, as well as grass-fed meat choices. It discourages the intake of highly processed foods that contain artificial colors and ingredients and promotes consuming foods that our ancestors ate, such as lean meats, fruits, vegetables, nuts, and seeds. A study has shown that this diet can help reduce thyroid antibodies and improve thyroid hormone levels. Following a Paleo diet rich in nutrient-dense whole foods, combined with lifestyle adjustments and specific supplements, can have a significant impact on thyroid health.

AIP (autoimmune protocol) lifestyle

This is a variation of the Paleo diet that focuses on removing specific foods, additives, and Western dietary habits that disrupt the balance of gut bacteria. Instead, this diet emphasizes the consumption of nutrient-rich whole foods.

While a recent study did not show a significant change in thyroid function or antibody levels, it did reveal a significant decrease in inflammation markers. This suggests that the autoimmune protocol (AIP) diet may help regulate immune and inflammatory responses in autoimmune thyroid disease.

For me personally, I have stuck to a gluten-free and mostly dairy-free diet; my only exception is a high quality cheese because I have not found a dairy-free cheese I like (IYKYK), and lots of whole foods! My diet is not quote on quote perfect but it is what works for me and has kept me in remission.

In summary, the food we consume has a significant influence on our bodily functions. It is evident that various vitamins and minerals not only affect thyroid health but also play crucial roles in bolstering the immune system, supporting liver functions, and regulating adrenal health. The timing, content, and manner of our eating are all significant factors. While research supports specific diets that can help manage Hashimoto's, it is important to remember that every individual is unique, and so are their specific nutrient needs. Therefore, it is necessary to *find what specifically works for you.* If the information feels overwhelming or challenging to apply, consider making changes gradually and *prioritize quality foods above all else.*

CHAPTER 7

Building a Foundation

*"Before you heal someone, ask him if
he is willing to give up the things that
make him sick." -Hippocrates*

Non-Toxic Living

Hopefully, as you become more attuned to your surroundings, you are also growing increasingly aware of how the things we encounter and consume impact our health and wellness. As discussed in previous chapters, toxins significantly affect our bodies. While we may not have control over farming practices, everyday pollution, or other people's habits, such as wearing perfume or smoking, we do have control over our home environment.

Personally, I didn't realize the value of my health until it reached a crisis point. Working the night shift led to erratic sleep patterns, with no structured morning or night routines. I often fell asleep to the TV or after scrolling mindlessly on my phone, and my eating habits were chaotic- either skipping meals due to busyness or consuming low-nutrient foods because they were quick and easy, leading to late-night snacking. Despite trying various forms of exercise like kayaking, rowing, half-marathons, and yoga, nothing seemed to stick for the long haul. I lacked effective stress management skills, often suppressing my emotions or dismissing them as normal. This routine is not one I would recommend.

For years now, my health has been the most valuable thing in my life, and it should be for you too. If you don't have your health, what do you have? That is why I make a conscious effort to maintain a non-toxic life. Adapting to this lifestyle change can feel daunting at first, but I urge you to take it one step at a time. Start by replacing one item at a time or switching to a non-toxic alternative when a product runs out. Establishing new habits for a healthier lifestyle requires consistency, so be patient with yourself. Embracing change gradually will help you stay on track and avoid reverting back to old habits.

Sleep

We all crave a good night's rest, don't we? Whether it is the demands of daily life or external distractions hindering our sleep, sleep deprivation affects our health negatively. Finding yourself tossing and turning in the still of the night, being unable to switch off your racing thoughts, or simply feeling fatigued yet wide awake can be frustrating. Recent studies have unveiled the intricate connections between insufficient sleep and various health disorders, such as a weakened immune system, mood disorders, neurodegenerative diseases, hypertension, cardiovascular disease, obesity, diabetes, and chronic loneliness, not to mention untreated thyroid dysfunction can greatly impact a person's ability to achieve restful and healthy sleep.

Experts recommend that most people aim for seven to seven and a half hours of sleep per night for optimal health, noting that continuous wakefulness exceeding sixteen hours can rapidly diminish cognitive performance and alertness. It is also important to remember that, much like the accumulation of daily toxins, sleep deficits build up over time. Sleep deprivation can lead to a significant deterioration in alertness. Developing a bedtime routine can be especially beneficial!

Morning routine

Starting the day with a nutritious breakfast can lead to a better intake of essential nutrients, a healthier body mass index, improved cognitive performance, and enhanced overall well-being. Additionally, consuming coffee can offer many health benefits, but the amount, quality (ensuring it is pesticide- and mycotoxin/mold-free), and timing (consuming it after you have eaten something first) of the caffeine intake are important. Meditation, as a formal practice, can help calm the mind and increase self-awareness. Making time to be outdoors—soaking up the sunlight, grounding your feet, and getting some exercise—can further enhance your morning routine. By customizing your morning activities to fit your preferences, you can set a positive tone for the rest of your day.

For me personally, I start my day with morning affirmations as I am getting ready. I then walk my dog to the park to play fetch. I also simultaneously am soaking up the morning sunlight, doing grounding work by standing barefoot in the fluffy green grass, and drinking my lemon water. I do not schedule any work or pick up any electronic devices during this time.

Exercise

From a young age, we have all been told about the importance of exercise and a healthy diet. Regular daily physical activity is one of the most potent lifestyle choices for enhancing cardiovascular and metabolic health. It also significantly improves fitness, mood, and cognitive function, while reducing the risk of mortality. Research indicates that regular exercise positively impacts overall health, including boosting the immune system, reducing inflammation, and improving hormone levels such as TSH and T4.

If you have hypothyroidism or Hashimoto's, you may often feel fatigued and too tired to exercise. It's completely valid to feel like you barely have enough energy to get through the day. As you may recall from earlier in the book, the primary function of thyroid hormones is to control metabolism. Therefore, if you have hypothyroidism, in which the body suffers from low metabolism, symptoms can include reduced energy expenditure, weight gain, impaired blood glucose regulation, elevated cholesterol levels, and decreased breakdown of fats into energy molecules. However, the solution is not to avoid exercise but to find the right type of exercise for you at this moment. It doesn't have to be strenuous activities like running or HIIT workouts; low-impact options like yoga and Pilates can be equally beneficial.

Activities like Pilates and yoga are particularly attractive due to their direct benefits on physical well-being, including weight management, enhanced posture, flexibility, and cardiovascular function. Interestingly, a study confirmed that participating in Pilates and yoga fosters healthy behaviors and cultivates a positive outlook on subjective health status, thereby initiating a cycle of positive reinforcement. The research provides solid evidence that promoting Pilates or yoga can be an effective intervention strategy to inspire individuals to make healthy lifestyle changes.

Note: *I highly recommend picking an exercise that makes you feel good and gives you more energy by the time you leave. When you love it, it is easy to stick with, and when you stick with it, you form a habit, until eventually it just becomes part of your weekly routine.*

I personally, have tried half marathons, rowing, biking, hiking, and yoga. They are great workouts and have many benefits but I could never stick with any of them. I would start and stay consistent for maybe six months and then want to move on. But I was always willing to *try* something new. That mindset is how I tried pilates and fell in love with it!

Circadian rhythm

Animals and plants, just like us, have their own internal clocks that help them stay in sync with the day-and-night cycle. Our internal clock has two important features: it naturally follows a 24-hour cycle, regardless of external conditions; and it can adjust its timing based on both light and non-light signals, which include sunlight, darkness, sound, exercise, meal times, and changes in temperature. But sometimes, like in the case of people who work night shifts (where my night nurses at?), our body clocks can get mixed up, leading to a mismatch between our sleep patterns and this natural timing system.

When everything is working normally, our behaviors and this biological timing system work together to keep our hormones in balance. Many hormones vary across the day and night, but let's take a closer look at cortisol and thyroid hormones:

- Cortisol is at its lowest in the evening, when we usually get ready for bed. It then quickly goes up in the middle of the night, when we are asleep, and reaches its highest point in the morning when we wake up.

- Thyroid-stimulating hormone (TSH) follows a specific daily pattern as well. The levels start to go up in the late afternoon and early evening, before we go to bed, and reach their highest point during the early part of the night. After this nighttime peak, TSH levels start to decrease for the rest of our sleeping time, reaching their lowest point in the daytime. Studies have shown that when people don't get enough sleep or when their sleep schedule suddenly changes, their TSH levels in the morning become twice as high compared to those who had a regular night of sleep.

Stress management

When we are stressed, our body releases a hormone called cortisol, which can impact how our thyroid gland functions. High cortisol levels from stress can lower our thyroid hormones, leading to hypothyroidism (remember in the beginning when my TSH dramatically escalated and my doctor thought it was an acute stress response? This is why!). Prolonged stress also weakens our immune system and creates more inflammation. This can exacerbate Hashimoto's autoimmune symptoms.

A study found that patients with Hashimoto's saw a 90% success rate in treatment of stress levels and thyroid symptoms by utilizing acupuncture as a stress-relieving technique and magnesium supplementation (only in those who showed low serum magnesium).

Note: *Other stress-relieving activities include meditation, hypno-breathwork, box breathing, alternate nostril breathing, exercise, journaling, coloring, doing puzzles, dancing, music, therapy, massages, saunas, red light therapy, getting out in nature and grounding yourself, basking in sunshine, taking a nap and a break, processing emotions, and playing with a pet.*

I recommend finding a few stress management tools that resonate with you and start incorporating them into your daily routine before reaching a point of burnout. Numerous obstacles can hinder the ease with which you can complete these tasks, from work commitments and parenting responsibilities to lack of motivation and physical limitations. These tools don't have to be burdensome tasks; they can be simple adjustments, like changing the music you listen to in the car on your way to work or during your morning routine. If you are viewing these practices as hard, complicated, or negative, I would challenge your mindset to consider how these practices can bring peace, joy, or laughter to your day. This perspective might help you embrace and utilize these practices more effectively.

In summary, without establishing a strong foundation for good health, how can you expect improvement in any aspect of your life? If you don't have your health, what do you have?

CHAPTER 8

The Mindset Shift:
Reshaping Beliefs

*"Wellness is the complete integration of body,
mind, and spirit— the realization that everything
we do, think, feel, and believe has an effect on
our state of well-being." - Greg Anderson*

Making changes to your health can be challenging, and often we falter because we desire simplicity. I too longed for an easy path, but when faced with a health crisis, I prioritized my well-being and vitality enough to commit to the arduous journey and persevere. I discovered that decisions flow effortlessly when they are in harmony with your true self. Conversely, engaging in tasks that do not resonate with your core values can prove exceptionally difficult. Therefore, it is important to deeply connect with your motivations when making choices to confidently move forward. Who wouldn't want to free themselves from the grip of Hashimoto's and avoid needless suffering? However, achieving remission requires a vision for a healthier and happier future, a commitment that starts today and must continue indefinitely.

THE CHANGE MINDSET

You can prevent chronic diseases by making healthy lifestyle choices, such as maintaining proper nutrition, engaging in regular physical activity, undergoing preventative screenings, and avoiding harmful habits like tobacco use and excessive alcohol consumption. Yet despite this clear path to prevention, many individuals fail to prioritize these essential steps. As a result, chronic diseases account for the majority of deaths in the United States. This raises the question: Why do people neglect these fundamental health practices?

Uncovering your motivation

I like to ask potential clients, "If you were given the answer *today* of how you can put your Hashimoto's into remission and live a happier, healthier life, would you commit to making the necessary changes?" While the response may seem obvious, our society often seeks instant gratification and quick fixes instead of embracing the long-term commitment required for lasting health.

Ultimately, breaking the cycle of illness and achieving sustainable wellness requires a shift in mindset from reactive measures to proactive, lasting lifestyle adjustments. It is crucial to understand the underlying motivations driving our choices—our "whys"—as they serve as a powerful force guiding us through the obstacles we encounter on our journey to better habits and behaviors. Embracing the "why" behind our health goals propels us toward meaningful change and empowers us to break free from the patterns that led to our initial health challenges.

You want to lose weight... *WHY?*

You want Hashimoto's remission... *WHY?*

You want to eat healthier... *WHY?*

You want to start exercising... *WHY?*

You want to get rid of the brain fog and fatigue... *WHY?*

You want a non-toxic life... *WHY?*

Personally, I was driven to unravel the puzzling mystery of my circumstances and understand why I was suddenly experiencing them. I was determined to break free from the incapacitating symptoms that hindered me from fulfilling my purpose and enjoying life.

While you might initially dismiss the idea as simplistic or obvious, it is crucial to recognize that surface-level responses like "because" or "it's healthy" are inadequate for setting meaningful goals. Your motivation—your why—must be deeply personal and rooted in your own desires and aspirations. It cannot be swayed by external pressures, such as seeking validation from others, following the crowd, or mimicking someone else's success story. Your why is uniquely yours. When embarking on a new endeavor or seeking to implement change, your mind will naturally resist, clinging to familiarity and comfort as a means of self-preservation. Your inner critic will quickly list all the reasons why you cannot succeed. Therefore, mental readiness is essential when facing significant transformations. Understand that no one else can do the work for you or dictate your path. The responsibility lies solely with you to pursue your goals and put in the necessary effort. Embracing change and confronting challenges head-on is inevitable as you progress toward your objectives. How you manage and navigate these obstacles will ultimately determine your success in any endeavor. Remember, it is your unwavering determination and dedication that will lead you to triumph, not external influences or directives. Your journey is yours to own, shape, and conquer.

Are you ready?

Now that you've gained clarity on the "why" behind your desire to improve your health and wellness, it's important to recognize what stage of change you are currently in.

The first stage is **contemplation**. This is when you are considering making changes but have not committed yet. You may be pondering how life would be *better* if you made a change.

The second stage is **preparation**. At this stage, you have decided you're going to make a change. You sit down and make a list of *your* barriers, e.g., "I don't have time," "Healthy habits cost too much," "I can't do this alone," or "I don't like eating healthy or exercising." Once you've identified these barriers, list out the solution for each of them. Start jotting down all your ideas and collecting all your resources to support your health goals.

The third stage is **acting**. Here, you are actively following the plan you created, overcoming obstacles and adjusting to this new lifestyle. You're reviewing your goals, making adjustments, planning for any setbacks you foresee, and celebrating your progress.

The fourth step is **maintenance**. You've established a new routine! You have been consistent for at least six months now; setbacks no longer discourage you, and you may be challenging yourself with new goals at this stage.

Set yourself up for success

We all have motives driving our actions. You can settle for superficial reasons that satisfy yourself and others, or you can dive deeper to uncover the core justification behind your choices. Discovering your authentic "why" is the potent force that sustains you through adversity, not just during triumphs. The moment you unearth your true motivation, you can map out how to attain your goals by establishing SMART goals. SMART stands for Specific, Measurable, Attainable, Realistic, and Timely.

The common pitfall that leads to veering off track or abandoning our aspirations is merely stating intentions without a concrete plan or solid reasoning. Saying, "I will run two miles daily to lose weight" is cute, but the goal is too vague and therefore runs the risk of failure. There is no way to evaluate progress; it doesn't list the possible barriers, it doesn't explain your WHY, and it doesn't include a deadline or a way to hold you accountable. It is vital to outline a clear roadmap with actionable steps to fuel your commitment and drive toward achievement.

If we were to take that vague goal and transform it into a SMART goal, it would look like this:

- **Specific**: I want to lose 10 pounds by running two miles every day for three months.

- **Measurable**: I will weigh in every two weeks using the scale in my bathroom.

- **Attainable**: I don't know if I can run two full miles, so I will start by running half a mile and walking the rest of the way for the first week. Every week, I will increase my running by another half mile. I might be tired some days and not feel like running; in these instances, I will evaluate if I can just walk it all or if I need to give my body a rest day. I will celebrate my small wins along the way, and I will give myself grace on the days that I cannot perform to the best of my ability.

- **Realistic/Relevant**: I am doing this to develop better health habits and to feel good about myself. This aligns with my values. I have the equipment I need, and I have made this goal a priority by putting it in my calendar every evening.

- **Timely**: I will complete my goal within three months.

My initial SMART goal in my health journey was to implement an elimination diet. I committed to adhering to this diet for a full three months before reintroducing foods, aiming to pinpoint my food sensitivities and reduce inflammation within my body. Uncertain about my ability to forgo numerous food categories, I resolved to show myself compassion in the face of any setbacks while striving to improve. With concerns about being hungry, I planned to prep my meals ahead of time. Whenever feelings of doubt crept in, I reminded myself that this process was temporary and that I would be adding back food categories before I knew it.

Don't think you could make changes to your lifestyle? Let's talk about that self-limiting mindset next.

SELF-LIMITING MINDSET

Are you getting in the way of your own health success?

Have you ever thought or been told the following ideas?

- That is impossible.

- I am not qualified enough for that.

- That is too expensive.

- That is too difficult.

- I couldn't do that even if I tried.

These limiting beliefs, whether they stem from external opinions or self-imposed doubts, serve as barriers to your progress. By allowing these voices of skepticism to influence your decisions, you unwittingly adopt other people's fears and beliefs as your own limitations. Instead of moving forward, you find yourself stuck before even attempting to make a change. Challenges are inevitable, but they only become insurmountable when you confine yourself to a narrative of impossibility or allow others to steer you in that direction. Every obstacle is an opportunity for growth and learning—a temporary barrier that you can navigate and overcome. Do not let these setbacks paralyze you or divert you from your path. Embrace the challenges as stepping stones on your journey to personal development and well-being.

What does your self-talk sound like? Is it a nurturing space that fosters growth, or do you find yourself being overly critical and unkind to yourself? This initial inquiry is important as you're embarking on a journey to enhance your health and well-being and your inner dialogue will be your constant companion. Do you desire a supportive and optimistic mindset that uplifts you or one that consistently undermines your confidence and leaves you feeling defeated?

Interacting with different mentors has taught me to become aware of my inner dialogue and to address the negative narrative. I have learned that whenever you have a negative thought about yourself—for instance, when you tell yourself things like "You idiot, why did you do that? Who the hell do you think you are? You can't do that!"—you are disparaging the person you should love and care about the most. If you can't look your most beloved person in the face and say those things to them, then you should not say them to yourself. My mentors challenged me to say these words to the person I love and respect the most. It remains one of the most impactful exercises I have ever undertaken. Tears welled up in my eyes as I contemplated speaking the words out loud to my husband. I felt like Ella in *Ella Enchanted*, compelled to unwillingly harm someone I loved, and the thought of verbalizing it was daunting. I found myself apologizing before uttering the words. When I finally muttered them out loud, the look of astonishment in my husband's eyes and his subsequent comment—"You are a bully to yourself!"—struck a chord within me. I realized how incredibly mean I was being to myself. I was harsher than anyone had ever been to me, and harsher than I would ever fathom being to anyone else. *We are truly our own worst critics.*

Note: *Be willing to give yourself grace, understanding, and love, because how you treat yourself sets the tone for how you allow others to treat you.*

Self-belief stems from recognizing your inherent worth as a human being, trusting yourself, and maintaining a positive perspective on your abilities and attributes. However, at times, our self-belief can become clouded by the messages from those around us. I used to push myself past my breaking point to complete tasks, even if it meant passing out. Why? Because not finishing meant I had failed, and that was unacceptable. Where did this belief come from? At some point in my life, I was taught that accomplishment equals worthiness. Therefore, my habit of pushing so hard for success was an attempt to prove that I was enough—for other people. I relied on others to validate my value, affirm that my skills and qualities were adequate, and confirm that I could be relied upon.

Note: *Ladies, if your self-belief, self-worth, and self-confidence are so easily shaken up by what others have to say about you, then I hate to burst your bubble, but you never had those things to begin with. True self-belief, self-worth, and self-confidence come from what you think and believe about yourself, regardless of what others have to say. They're unshakable, undeniable, unwavering. No one can take away something that is inherently yours to hold.*

At times, our actions and decisions are driven by subconscious beliefs instilled in us through past experiences. Perhaps your managers repeatedly overlooked you for leadership roles, leading you to internalize the belief that you lack leadership abilities and consequently turn down leadership opportunities when they arise. Maybe a family member dismissed your dreams as unattainable, or a doctor delivered a discouraging diagnosis without exploring alternative options. Have you ever convinced yourself that aiming high is foolish and that you should stick to what you know? Or have you encountered remarks suggesting that only certain individuals can attain wealth or that certain jobs are off-limits? These subtle messages can shape our beliefs and influence our choices, often without us realizing their impact.

Understanding the origins of your beliefs and values is crucial, especially when it comes to making changes in habits or behaviors, as you will need support. It's vital to ensure that this support comes from the right individuals and aligns with the right mindset. Becoming your own greatest supporter may require a shift in how you perceive yourself. By deeply exploring your core identity, desires, values, and beliefs, you can make decisions that truly resonate with your authentic self. This alignment fuels your motivation and propels you toward success in any endeavor you aspire to achieve.

But perhaps delving into the origins of your beliefs, particularly if rooted in trauma, and exploring your core identity, desires, and values, can appear challenging because of the survival mindset you have created to protect yourself.

Note: *you are growing and it is safe to grow.*

SURVIVAL MINDSET

Despite enduring numerous hardships, I have always found the strength to rise again and persevere. Sister tried to drown me? I survived. Car accident? I survived. Bullied in school? I survived. Threatened and abused? I survived. Crashed into a tree while downhill skiing? I survived. Kidney stones during college finals? I survived. Worked the front line during a pandemic? I survived. Personal health crisis? I survived. Do you know what all of these have in common? **Survival mindset.**

Note: *I would like you to take a brief pause here. Place your left hand on your heart and your right hand on your stomach. Let's take a couple of deep breaths, in and out. It's okay. You're safe. I got you. I know some of those words can be very triggering and that not everyone survives. It's okay to take a minute and hold space for that. What does your heart need to hear?*

My family did not grow up rich. We were a house of seven, with six of us being girls! Like all siblings, we fought and sought to destroy each other, all in good fun. We moved around a bit, and I remember this one particular day, my mom had gotten me to a new school a bit late that first day, so when the principal walked me to my class, everyone turned around and stared at me. Cue teenage embarrassment and eyes of judgment as you sink into your chair in the back of the room.

Despite feeling out of place at times, I approached each new environment with determination and a focus on my studies. Unfortunately, I was picked on, just like many other kids. Kids at school were relentless in their teasing, targeting me for not wearing name-brand clothes and making fun of my appearance. They would ridicule my small eyes and criticize my pale skin at a time when tanning was all the rage. As a result, I always made sure to cover up, opting for long sleeves and pants, even in hot weather. During classes, I would sit uneasily in my long sleeves, enduring the stifling heat. For gym and sports, I wore long basketball shorts to avoid drawing attention to my body. One time, a parent rumored that I had stolen a pair of her daughter's Spanx. The false rumor circulated, causing anxiety for a teenage girl who lacked confidence in her appearance.

Looking back as an adult, I can't help but chuckle at the memory, knowing that I wasn't secure enough to wear such clothing. There was a moment in my junior year when someone asked me to prom, but I declined. My lack of body confidence and uncertainty about affording a dress held me back, highlighting the deep insecurity I felt at the time. I didn't want to "be seen." Lost in a mire of self-doubt and unworthiness, I internalized the torment, molding their harmful words into a self-imposed narrative of inadequacy and insignificance.

Struggling in silence, devoid of parental support or community guidance, I found no refuge from the harsh judgments that permeated my small town. The absence of a supportive voice highlighting my strengths and worth left me feeling inadequate and unsafe in a world where cruelty seemed prevalent.

Note: *A study revealed that experiencing childhood traumatic stress, such as physical, emotional, or sexual abuse, witnessing domestic violence, parental divorce, or growing up in a household with substance abuse, can increase the chances of being diagnosed with an autoimmune disease in adulthood! This information reinforces the concept, as reiterated in the beginning chapters, that every single experience we encounter from birth until now has a profound impact on our health.*

All I had was my work, and I excelled in that—it was my superpower, but it also fueled my low self-worth. This left me to continuously pressure myself in every situation to do and be better, both in school and outside of school. Until one day, during a talk therapy session, my therapist posed this question: *"What are you striving for, deep down?"*

It dawned on me that I was seeking other people's approval and acceptance and yearning to be seen as someone worthy. What they don't tell you is that vocalizing this desire is the most challenging step. It's a testament to your pain, hurt, and loss of identity. We have all gone through things. Hard things. We all try to put our heads down and develop a way to deal with things. But why? We are human beings, complex beings, and just like the digestive tract, we need to process things in order to get them out and feel better (pun intended).

Before you pass judgment on me for seeking therapy, I want to emphasize that I truly believe everyone could benefit from seeing a therapist. As I mentioned above, we are complex beings with our own unique stories and challenges. Unfortunately, school did not teach us a lot about how to process the endless emotions and problems we could and would come to face at some point during our lives.

Believe it or not, over 35 million US children have experienced childhood trauma, which leads to—yes, you guessed it—a host of emotional and psychological problems that are not properly identified, expressed, or managed.

You can probably think of a few individuals who seem to hold grudges and struggle to let things go—so can I. Ultimately, we all crave understanding, love, and a chance to be heard. There is often a negative stigma associated with seeking therapy because of the belief that one must be severely troubled to require that level of assistance. Here's a reality check for you: you don't have to be completely broken to benefit from therapy. Therapists are compassionate professionals who have dedicated themselves to helping others navigate life's challenges. They provide invaluable support by creating a safe space for processing emotions, asking the right questions to shift negative mindsets toward positivity, offering practical tools for daily coping, and allowing the time needed for healing and personal growth. It's essential to recognize that difficulties are not exclusive to specific groups of people—we all have problems and yearn for someone to truly listen.

Note: *The real question is, are you brave enough to ask for help and set yourself free from your emotional burden? And before you say no, ask yourself if you are the only one suffering. Are there people around you who are also suffering from the way you treat them because of the unresolved issues you're struggling to confront? Or are they suffering from having to watch you go through it and not deal with it in a healthy way?*

My therapist has been instrumental in guiding my personal healing journey by helping me uncover my true identity, allowing me to discover my genuine passions, and facilitating the shift from negative to positive thinking. This transformation necessitates a steadfast commitment and does not happen overnight because, as you know, healing takes time. Most importantly, she taught me how important I am as a human being and that I am worthy of all the love and kindness that I give so freely to everyone else. While I have tackled formidable challenges, the toughest and most profound work

I have ever undertaken revolves around learning to love and value myself. This realization, that my worthiness is intrinsic and cannot be bestowed or stripped away by others, brought even my husband to tears as he expressed his immense pride in witnessing this pivotal growth moment. He recognized the profound impact of this breakthrough, having observed my inner torment for years as I struggled to believe **I was important, worthy, good enough, smart enough, beautiful enough, and successful enough** for anything or anyone.

In life, there will always be individuals—whether they are family members, friends, or fleeting acquaintances—who have the power to say or do things that can leave you feeling unworthy and hurt. It is important to recognize that by allowing their negative actions and words to affect you, you are relinquishing your power to determine your self-worth to them. Instead of spiraling into a cycle of negativity and self-doubt each time someone treats you poorly, consider questioning why they might be acting that way. It is crucial to acknowledge that everyone carries their own pain and struggles differently. As the saying goes, those who are mean often need the most love.

The survival mindset can hinder personal growth and negatively impact health. Maslow's hierarchy of needs highlights the importance of fulfilling basic human needs as a foundation for well-being. Starting with essentials, such as food, water, air, and shelter, and progressing to safety, security, and health, these fundamental requirements must be met to advance to higher levels of fulfillment. Feeling secure is crucial for addressing subsequent needs like love and belonging, esteem, and self-actualization. When we continually feel unsafe, our fight-or-flight hormones are constantly released, causing chronic low-level inflammation and wreaking havoc on our health.

Studies show that both psychological and physical stressors can lead to immunological changes, potentially contributing to autoimmune disorders and other health issues. Stress affects the immune system, either directly or indirectly, through the nervous and endocrine systems. These immune modulations may contribute to the development of autoimmunity and increase susceptibility to autoimmune diseases in genetically predisposed individuals, highlighting the significant impact of environmental factors on health outcomes.

Note: *There are some amazing tools and resources out there for trauma support and healing: talk therapy, trauma coaches, somatic coaches, energy healers, journaling, meditation, and more! As you can see from reading the above research, trauma impacts your health too, so if living your best life and enjoying optimal health and wellness is your goal, addressing your trauma should be a part of that journey.*

To conclude, which mindset do you feel is where you are right now in your jouney? Are you in the change mindset? Self-limiting mindset? Or the survival mindset? If you are unsure I would take some time and identify which mindset you are in. This is important because you cannot heal in survival mode, you cannot heal if you don't believe you can, and you cannot heal if you aren't ready to make the changes necessary. It's important to be honest with yourself here because it will impact your success with your health goals.

Know that mindset work doesn't have an expiration date. It's not expected of you to say, "okay, in 3 months I won't be in survival mode or in 6 months I will believe in myself". Mindset work is an ongoing process, involving both old and new challenges. Don't let it be this barrier keeping you from your health journey, aka don't wait for everything to be "perfect" before you begin. Healing our body, mind, and spirit all take time; it is not a destination, it is a way of life.

Note: *don't skip the mindset work*

CONCLUSION

*E*verything you have been exposed to and experienced in your life, has shaped your health!

That is why it is so important to take a look at the whole picture- by identifying your triggers and root causes you can eliminate them and support your body's healing processes -to restore the body back to balance.

Thyroid health goes beyond the thyroid and medication.

I understand the challenges and frustrations that come with advocating for oneself in healthcare. The journey of seeking answers, trying different providers and treatment avenues, and feeling unheard or dismissed is a common experience for many individuals navigating health issues. The emotional toll of being repeatedly told that nothing is wrong or being offered oversimplified solutions can lead to feelings of hopelessness and isolation.

The truth is, advocating for oneself in the realm of healthcare can be a challenging journey, riddled with dismissals, misdiagnoses, and feelings of being unheard. This experience can leave individuals questioning the validity of their own experiences. It is okay to seek out different providers, conduct personal research, and explore alternative care routes to find the answers and support needed for one's health.

It is also crucial to acknowledge the gaps and shortcomings in our current healthcare system, particularly in the realm of thyroid health and conditions such as Hashimoto's. The importance of thyroid hormones cannot be underestimated, as they have a profound impact on the body as a whole. It is evident that a more personalized and comprehensive approach to thyroid care is necessary, one that goes beyond simply prescribing synthetic hormone medications.

While progress and change within the healthcare system may be slow, it is important to remain patient and hopeful that advancements are being made. By sharing our stories and experiences, we not only validate our own journeys but also have the potential to help others who may be facing similar challenges. Ultimately, understanding that our health and well-being matter and that we are not alone in our struggles can be a powerful source of empowerment and solidarity in the face of adversity.

In addition, bridging the gap in thyroid and autoimmune disease care can be effectively achieved by incorporating a functional medicine practitioner into your healthcare team. These practitioners specialize in investigating the root causes of health issues, creating personalized treatment plans, and addressing the body as a whole. By working in tandem with health coaches, they can provide comprehensive support and guidance to help patients implement necessary changes for improved health outcomes.

It is important to recognize that both traditional medical approaches and functional medicine have valuable contributions to offer and they can be complementary rather than exclusive. Integrating both systems can lead to better patient outcomes.

But ultimately, the power to drive your health journey rests in your hands. Remember that you have the autonomy to select your healthcare team, make informed choices about your treatment options, and take proactive steps towards your health and wellness goals. By incorporating lifestyle changes, proper nutrition, and personalized care, you can actively work towards achieving remission and managing thyroid and autoimmune conditions effectively.

In sharing my own journey towards seeking functional medicine, I hope to offer guidance and support to those facing similar challenges. By recognizing the importance of individualized care, understanding the impact of thyroid health on overall well-being, and staying informed about the latest research and developments, we can collectively work towards improving the quality of care for thyroid and autoimmune conditions. While my personal experience sheds light on some aspects of Hashimoto's and thyroid health, there is a vast amount of information and resources available to further support individuals on their health journeys. To explore more about triggers, root causes, nutrition, and lifestyle practices related to Hashimoto's, I invite you to join Love, Your Thyroid™ for additional insights and guidance. Remember, you are not alone in this journey, and there are steps you can take *today* to shift towards a path of healing and well-being.

REFERENCES

Chapter 2

(2024, January 1). *ABIM Laboratory Test Reference Ranges.* American Board of Internal Medicine. https://www. abim.org/Media/bfijryql/laboratory-reference-ranges. pdf

Bunch, D., PhD, DABCC (2021, July 1). *Modern Reference Intervals.* Association for Diagnostics and Laboratory Medicine. https://www.myadlm.org/cln/articles/2021/ july/modern-reference-intervals

Cleveland Clinic. (2024). *Hashimoto's Disease.* Cleveland Clinic. https://my.clevelandclinic.org/health/ diseases/17665-hashimotos-disease

Cleveland Clinic. (2024). *Thyroid Hormone.* Cleveland Clinic. https://my.clevelandclinic.org/health/ articles/22391-thyroid-hormone

Cleveland Clinic. (2024). *Hypothyroidism.* Cleveland Clinic. https://my.clevelandclinic.org/health/ diseases/12120-hypothyroidism

Klubo-Gwiezdzinska, J., & Wartofsky, L. (2022). Hashimoto thyroiditis: An evidence-based guide to etiology, diagnosis and treatment. *Polish Archives of Internal Medicine, 132*(3). https://doi.org/10.20452/pamw.16222

Shomon, M. (2023, June 8). *Factors That Can Affect Thyroid Test Results.* VeryWell Health. https://www.verywellhealth.com/optimum-time-and-conditions-for-thyroid-blood-tests-3232911#:~:text=Some%20medications%20can%20alter%20thyroid%20hormone%20function%20and,kinase%20inhibitors%2C%20like%20Nexavar%20%28sorafenib%29%20or%20Sutent%20%28sunitinib%29

(n.d.). *Synthroid.* Synthroid. https://www.synthroid.com/?cid=ppc_ppd_MSFT_Synthroid_Branded_synthroid_Exact_USSYNT210334&&msclkid=746aa877473619a6f9ffcddab822bb84&gclid=746aa877473619a6f9ffcddab822bb84&gclsrc=3p.ds

Wiersinga, W. M., MD, PhD (2018, April 25). *Myxedema and Coma (Severe Hypothyroidism).* National Library of Medicine. https://www.ncbi.nlm.nih.gov/books/NBK279007/

Chapter 3

Bartemus, J., Dr. (2020). *The Autoimmune Answer* (1st ed.). Best Seller Publishing LLC.

Chu, B., Marwaha, K., Sanvictores, T., & Ayers, D. (2022, September 12). *Physiology, Stress Reaction*. National Library of Medicine. https://www.ncbi.nlm.nih.gov/books/NBK541120/

Colen, C. G., & Ramey, D. M. (2014). Is Breast Truly Best? Estimating the Effect of Breastfeeding on Long-term Child Wellbeing in the United States Using Sibling Comparisons. *Social Science & Medicine (1982), 109*, 55. https://doi.org/10.1016/j.socscimed.2014.01.027

Drageset, J. (2021, March 12). *Social Support*. National Library of Medicine. https://www.ncbi.nlm.nih.gov/books/NBK585650/

Harvard Medical School (2024, April 3). *Understanding the Stress Response*. Harvard Health Publishing. http://health.harvard.edu/staying-healthy/understanding-the-stress-response

Hanscom, M., Loane, D. J., & Shea-Donohue, T. (2021). Brain-gut axis dysfunction in the pathogenesis of traumatic brain injury. *The Journal of clinical investigation, 131*(12), e143777. https://doi.org/10.1172/JCI143777

(2019, April 23). *Social isolation, loneliness in older people pose health risks.* National Institute on Aging. https://www.nia.nih.gov/news/ social-isolation-loneliness-older-people-pose-health-risks

(2024, February). *Caring for Your Mental Health.* National Institute of Mental Health. https://www.nimh.nih.gov/ health/topics/caring-for-your-mental-health

Neu, J., & Rushing, J. (2011). Cesarean versus Vaginal Delivery: Long-term infant outcomes and the Hygiene Hypothesis. *Clinics in Perinatology, 38*(2), 321. https:// doi.org/10.1016/j.clp.2011.03.008

Nichol, J. R., Sundjaja, J. H., & Nelson, G. (2023, September 4). *Medical History.* National Library of Medicine. https://www.ncbi.nlm.nih.gov/books/ NBK534249/

Shi, Z. (2019). Gut Microbiota: An Important Link between Western Diet and Chronic Diseases. *Nutrients, 11*(10). https://doi.org/10.3390/nu11102287

Stuebe, A. (2009). The Risks of Not Breastfeeding for Mothers and Infants. *Reviews in Obstetrics and Gynecology, 2*(4), 222-231. https://www.ncbi.nlm.nih. gov/pmc/articles/PMC2812877/

Substance Abuse and Mental Health Services Administration (2014, March). *Understanding the Impact of Trauma.* National Library of Medicine. https://www.ncbi.nlm. nih.gov/books/NBK207191/

Totsch, S., Quinn, T., Strath, L., McMeekin, L., Cowell, R., Gower, B. & Sorge, R. (2017). The impact of the Standard American Diet in rats: Effects on behavior, physiology and recovery from inflammatory injury. *Scandinavian Journal of Pain*, *17*(1), 316-324. https://doi.org/10.1016/j.sjpain.2017.08.009

Zhang, P. (2022). Influence of Foods and Nutrition on the Gut Microbiome and Implications for Intestinal Health. *International Journal of Molecular Sciences*, *23*(17). https://doi.org/10.3390/ijms23179588

Chapter 4

Aghili R, Jafarzadeh F, Ghorbani R, Khamseh ME, Salami MA, Malek M. The association of *Helicobacter pylori* infection with Hashimoto's thyroiditis. Acta Med Iran. 2013 May 30;51(5):293-6. PMID: 23737311.

Appunni, S., Rubens, M., Ramamoorthy, V., Saxena, A., Tonse, R., Veledar, E., & McGranaghan, P. (2021). Association between vitamin D deficiency and hypothyroidism: results from the National Health and Nutrition Examination Survey (NHANES) 2007-2012. *BMC endocrine disorders*, *21*(1), 224. https://doi.org/10.1186/s12902-021-00897-1

Benites-Zapata, V. A., Ignacio-Cconchoy, F. L., Ulloque-Badaracco, J. R., Hernandez-Bustamante, E. A., Alarcón-Braga, E. A., & Herrera-Añazco, P. (2023). Vitamin B12 levels in thyroid disorders: A systematic review and meta-analysis. *Frontiers in Endocrinology, 14.* https://doi.org/10.3389/fendo.2023.1070592

Bischoff, S. C., Barbara, G., Buurman, W., Ockhuizen, T., Schulzke, D., Serino, M., Tilg, H., Watson, A., & Wells, J. M. (2014). Intestinal permeability – a new target for disease prevention and therapy. *BMC Gastroenterology, 14.* https://doi.org/10.1186/s12876-014-0189-7

Buha, A., Matovic, V., Antonijevic, B., Bulat, Z., Curcic, M., Renieri, E. A., Tsatsakis, A. M., Schweitzer, A., & Wallace, D. (2018). Overview of Cadmium Thyroid Disrupting Effects and Mechanisms. *International Journal of Molecular Sciences, 19*(5). https://doi.org/10.3390/ijms19051501

Camilleri, M. (2019). The Leaky Gut: Mechanisms, Measurement and Clinical Implications in Humans. *Gut, 68*(8), 1516. https://doi.org/10.1136/gutjnl-2019-318427

Cleveland Clinic. (2024). *Calcitonin.* https://my.clevelandclinic.org/health/articles/22330-calcitonin

Cleveland Clinic (n.d.). *Vitamin B-12 Deficiency.* https://my.clevelandclinic.org/health/diseases/22831-vitamin-b12-deficiency

Dittfeld, A., Gwizdek, K., Michalski, M., & Wojnicz, R. (2016). A possible link between the Epstein-Barr virus infection and autoimmune thyroid disorders. *Central-*

European Journal of Immunology, 41(3), 297-301.
https://doi.org/10.5114/ceji.2016.63130

Dore, M. P., Fanciulli, G., Manca, A., & Pes, G. M.
(2023). Association of *Helicobacter pylori* Infection
with Autoimmune Thyroid Disease in the Female Sex.
Journal of Clinical Medicine, 12(15), 5150. https://doi.
org/10.3390/jcm12155150

Dunlap DB. Thyroid Function Tests. In: Walker HK, Hall
WD, Hurst JW, editors. Clinical Methods: The History,
Physical, and Laboratory Examinations. 3rd ed. Boston:
Butterworths; 1990. Chapter 142. PMID: 21250093

Evexia Diagnostics (n.d.). *GI-Map (GI Microbial Assay Plus).*
https://www.evexiadiagnostics.com/test-menu/gi-map-
gi-microbial-assay-plus/#:~:text=The%20GI-MAP%20
%28Microbial%20Assay%20Plus%29%20is%20
unique%20in,targeting%20the%20specific%20
DNA%20of%20the%20organisms%20tested

Garofalo, V., Condorelli, R. A., Cannarella, R., Aversa, A.,
Calogero, A. E., & Vignera, S. L. (2023). Relationship
between Iron Deficiency and Thyroid Function: A
Systematic Review and Meta-Analysis. *Nutrients,
15*(22). https://doi.org/10.3390/nu15224790

Halsall, D. J., & Oddy, S. (2020). Clinical and laboratory
aspects of 3,3′,5′-triiodothyronine (reverse T3).
Annals of Clinical Biochemistry. https://doi.
org/10.1177/0004563220969150

Hofer U. Fungal Pathogenesis: Candida's toxic relationship with its host. Nat Rev Microbiol. 2016 Apr;14(5):268. doi: 10.1038/nrmicro.2016.53. Epub 2016 Apr 12. PMID: 27067400

Hutfless S, Matos P, Talor MV, Caturegli P, Rose NR. Significance of prediagnostic thyroid antibodies in women with autoimmune thyroid disease. J Clin Endocrinol Metab. 2011 Sep;96(9):E1466-71. doi: 10.1210/jc.2011-0228. Epub 2011 Jun 29. PMID: 21715532; PMCID: PMC3167665

Klubo-Gwiezdzinska, J., & Wartofsky, L. (2022). Hashimoto thyroiditis: An evidence-based guide to etiology, diagnosis and treatment. *Polish Archives of Internal Medicine*, *132*(3). https://doi.org/10.20452/pamw.16222

Knezevic, J., Starchl, C., Berisha, A. T., & Amrein, K. (2020). Thyroid-Gut-Axis: How Does the Microbiota Influence Thyroid Function? *Nutrients*, *12*(6). https://doi.org/10.3390/nu12061769

Lammers, K. M., Lu, R., Brownley, J., Lu, B., Gerard, C., Thomas, K., Rallabhandi, P., Shea-Donohue, T., Tamiz, A., Alkan, S., Netzel-Arnett, S., Antalis, T., Vogel, S. N., & Fasano, A. (2008). Gliadin Induces an Increase in Intestinal Permeability and Zonulin Release by Binding to the Chemokine Receptor CXCR3. *Gastroenterology*, *135*(1), 194. https://doi.org/10.1053/j.gastro.2008.03.023

Lauritano EC, Bilotta AL, Gabrielli M, Scarpellini E, Lupascu A, Laginestra A, Novi M, Sottili S, Serricchio M, Cammarota G, Gasbarrini G, Pontecorvi A, Gasbarrini A. Association between hypothyroidism and small intestinal bacterial overgrowth. J Clin Endocrinol Metab. 2007 Nov;92(11):4180-4. doi: 10.1210/jc.2007-0606. Epub 2007 Aug 14. PMID: 17698907.

Lehmann HW, Lutterbüse N, Plentz A, Akkurt I, Albers N, Hauffa BP, Hiort O, Schoenau E, Modrow S. Association of parvovirus B19 infection and Hashimoto's thyroiditis in children. Viral Immunol. 2008 Sep;21(3):379-83. doi: 10.1089/vim.2008.0001. PMID: 18788945.

Mantis, N. J., Rol, N., & Corthésy, B. (2011). Secretory IgA's Complex Roles in Immunity and Mucosal Homeostasis in the Gut. *Mucosal Immunology, 4*(6), 603. https://doi.org/10.1038/mi.2011.41

Poliandri, A. H., Cabilla, J. P., Velardez, M. O., Bodo, C. C., & Duvilanski, B. H. (2003). Cadmium induces apoptosis in anterior pituitary cells that can be reversed by treatment with antioxidants. *Toxicology and applied pharmacology, 190*(1), 17–24. https://doi.org/10.1016/s0041-008x(03)00191-1

Prasad VD, Suresh E, Ramana GV. Assessment of Iron, Ferritin, TIBC and LDH levels a cross sectional study in Hypothyroid patients. **Int J Clin Biochem Res** 2020;7(4):458-460

Rajič B, Arapović J, Raguž K, Bošković M, Babić SM, Maslać S. Eradication of *Blastocystis hominis* prevents the development of symptomatic Hashimoto's thyroiditis: a case report. J Infect Dev Ctries. 2015 Jul 30;9(7):788-91. doi: 10.3855/jidc.4851. PMID: 26230132.

Soh, B., & Aw, C. (2019). Laboratory Testing in Thyroid Conditions - Pitfalls and Clinical Utility. *Annals of Laboratory Medicine*, *39*(1), 3-14. https://doi. org/10.3343/alm.2019.39.1.3

Tchounwou, P. B., Yedjou, C. G., Patlolla, A. K., & Sutton, D. J. (2012). Heavy Metals Toxicity and the Environment. *EXS*, *101*, 133. https://doi. org/10.1007/978-3-7643-8340-4_6

Thyroid Function Tests. American Thyroid Association. https://www.thyroid.org/thyroid-function-tests/

Wentz, I., PharmD, FASCP, & Nowosadzka, M., MD (2013). *Hashimoto's Thyroiditis Lifestyle Interventions for Finding and Treating the Root Cause* (1st ed.). Wentz LLC.

Chapter 5

Agency for Toxic Substances and Disease Registry (2011, November 28). *ToxFAQs™ for Atrazine*. CDC. https:// wwwn.cdc.gov/TSP/ToxFAQs/ToxFAQsDetails. aspx?faqid=854&toxid=59#:~:text=Top%20of%20 Page-,How%20can%20atrazine%20affect%20

my%20health%3F,of%20specific%20biological%20
differences%20between%20humans%20and%20
these%20types%20of%20animals

Azzouz LL, Sharma S. Physiology, Large Intestine. [Updated
2023 Jul 31]. In: StatPearls [Internet]. Treasure Island
(FL): StatPearls Publishing; 2024 Jan-. Available from:
https://www.ncbi.nlm.nih.gov/books/NBK507857/

Bauer, B. A., M.D. (2023, March 24). *What is BPA,
and what are the concerns about BPA?* Mayo Clinic.
https://www.mayoclinic.org/healthy-lifestyle/
nutrition-and-healthy-eating/expert-answers/bpa/faq-
20058331#:~:text=Exposure%20to%20BPA%20is%20
a,2%20diabetes%20and%20cardiovascular%20disease

Buttler (2015, November 25). *Health Hazards in
Common Home Products.* Northwest National
Medicine. https://nwnaturalmedicine.com/
health-hazards-in-common-home-products/

Chen, A., Kim, S. S., Chung, E., & Dietrich, K. N. (2013).
Thyroid Hormones in Relation to Lead, Mercury,
and Cadmium Exposure in the National Health
and Nutrition Examination Survey, 2007–2008.
Environmental Health Perspectives, 121(2), 181-186.
https://doi.org/10.1289/ehp.1205239

Chen, S. C., Liao, T. L., Wei, Y. H., Tzeng, C. R., & Kao,
S. H. (2010). Endocrine disruptor, dioxin (TCDD)-
induced mitochondrial dysfunction and apoptosis in
human trophoblast-like JAR cells. *Molecular human*

reproduction, *16*(5), 361–372. https://doi.org/10.1093/molehr/gaq004

Cleveland Clinic (2024). *Hypercapnia.* https://my.clevelandclinic.org/health/diseases/24808-hypercapnia

Cleveland Clinic (2024). *Kidney.* https://my.clevelandclinic.org/health/body/21824-kidney

Cleveland Clinic (2024). *Liver.* https://my.clevelandclinic.org/health/articles/21481-liver

Danailova, Y., Velikova, T., Nikolaev, G., Mitova, Z., Shinkov, A., Gagov, H., & Konakchieva, R. (2022). Nutritional Management of Thyroiditis of Hashimoto. *International Journal of Molecular Sciences*, *23*(9). https://doi.org/10.3390/ijms23095144

Emmanuel, U. C., Chukwudi, M. I., Monday, S. S., & Anthony, A. I. (2022). Human health risk assessment of heavy metals in drinking water sources in three senatorial districts of Anambra State, Nigeria. *Toxicology Reports*, *9*, 869-875. https://doi.org/10.1016/j.toxrep.2022.04.011

(2004, December 15). *Exposures add up – Survey results.* Environmental Working Group. https://www.ewg.org/news-insights/news/2004/12/exposures-add-survey-results

InformedHealth.org [Internet]. Cologne, Germany: Institute for Quality and Efficiency in Health Care (IQWiG);

2006-. In brief: How does the liver work? [Updated 2023 Feb 28]. Available from: https://www.ncbi.nlm.nih.gov/books/NBK279393/

Kheradpisheh, Z., Mirzaei, M., Mahvi, A. H., Mokhtari, M., Azizi, R., Fallahzadeh, H., & Ehrampoush, M. H. (2018). Impact of Drinking Water Fluoride on Human Thyroid Hormones: A Case-Control Study. *Scientific Reports*, *8*. https://doi.org/10.1038/s41598-018-20696-4

Martinez-Finley, E. J., & Aschner, M. (2014). Recent Advances in Mercury Research. *Current Environmental Health Reports*, *1*(2), 163. https://doi.org/10.1007/s40572-014-0014-z

Miller, C. (2020, September 1). *Human Biology: Organs of Excretion*. Thompson Rivers University. https://humanbiology.pressbooks.tru.ca/chapter/18-2-organs-of-excretion/#:~:text=The%20skin%20plays%20a%20role,a%20byproduct%20of%20protein%20catabolism

Myers, I. (2024, February 29). *EWG's Dirty Dozen Guide to Food Chemicals: The top 12 to avoid*. Environmental Working Group. https://www.ewg.org/consumer-guides/ewgs-dirty-dozen-guide-food-chemicals-top-12-avoid

(2024, April 2). *Endocrine Disruptors*. National Institute of Environmental Health Sciences. https://www.niehs.nih.gov/health/topics/agents/endocrine

Ostrowska, L., Gier, D., & Zyśk, B. (2021). The Influence of Reducing Diets on Changes in Thyroid Parameters in Women Suffering from Obesity and Hashimoto's Disease. *Nutrients*, *13*(3). https://doi.org/10.3390/nu13030862

Steinemann, A. (2016). Fragranced consumer products: Exposures and effects from emissions. *Air Quality, Atmosphere, & Health*, *9*(8), 861-866. https://doi.org/10.1007/s11869-016-0442-z

Tchounwou, P. B., Yedjou, C. G., Patlolla, A. K., & Sutton, D. J. (2012). Heavy Metals Toxicity and the Environment. *EXS*, *101*, 133. https://doi.org/10.1007/978-3-7643-8340-4_6

Wentz, I., PharmD, FASCP (2023, June 9). *Food Sensitivities and Hashimoto's*. Thyroid Pharmacist. https://thyroidpharmacist.com/articles/food-sensitivities-and-hashimotos/

Wentz, I., PharmD, FASCP (2017). *Hashimoto's Protocol: A 90 Day Plan for Reversing Thyroid Symptoms and Getting Your Life Back* (1st ed.). HarperOne.

Zhai, Q., Narbad, A., & Chen, W. (2015). Dietary Strategies for the Treatment of Cadmium and Lead Toxicity. *Nutrients*, *7*(1), 552-571. https://doi.org/10.3390/nu7010552

Chapter 6

Al Alawi, A. M., Al Badi, A., Al Huraizi, A., & Falhammar, H. (2021). Magnesium: The recent research and developments. *Advances in food and nutrition research*, *96*, 193–218. https://doi.org/10.1016/bs.afnr.2021.01.001

Aleman, R. S., Moncada, M., & Aryana, K. J. (2023). Leaky Gut and the Ingredients That Help Treat It: A Review. *Molecules*, *28*(2). https://doi.org/10.3390/molecules28020619

Ali Khan, S. Z., Lungba, R. M., Ajibawo-Aganbi, U., Veliginti, S., Perez Bastidas, M. V., Saleem, S., & Cancarevic, I. (2020). Minerals: An Untapped Remedy for Autoimmune Hypothyroidism? *Cureus*, *12*(10). https://doi.org/10.7759/cureus.11008

Ali Khan, S. Z., Lungba, R. M., Ajibawo-Aganbi, U., Veliginti, S., Perez Bastidas, M. V., Saleem, S., & Cancarevic, I. (2020). Minerals: An Untapped Remedy for Autoimmune Hypothyroidism? *Cureus*, *12*(10). https://doi.org/10.7759/cureus.11008

Abbaspour, N., Hurrell, R., & Kelishadi, R. (2014). Review on iron and its importance for human health. *Journal of Research in Medical Sciences : The Official Journal of Isfahan University of Medical Sciences*, *19*(2), 164-174. https://www.ncbi.nlm.nih.gov/pmc/articles/PMC3999603

Abbott, R. D., Sadowski, A., & Alt, A. G. (2019). Efficacy of the Autoimmune Protocol Diet as Part of a Multi-disciplinary, Supported Lifestyle Intervention for Hashimoto's Thyroiditis. *Cureus, 11*(4). https://doi.org/10.7759/cureus.4556

Ashok, T., Patni, N., Fatima, M., Lamis, A., & Siddiqui, S. W. (2022). Celiac Disease and Autoimmune Thyroid Disease: The Two Peas in a Pod. *Cureus, 14*(6). https://doi.org/10.7759/cureus.26243

Aslam, H., Green, J., Jacka, F. N., Collier, F., Berk, M., Pasco, J., & Dawson, S. L. (2020). Fermented foods, the gut and mental health: a mechanistic overview with implications for depression and anxiety. *Nutritional neuroscience, 23*(9), 659–671. https://doi.org/10.1080/1028415X.2018.1544332

Bellastella, G., Scappaticcio, L., Caiazzo, F., Tomasuolo, M., Carotenuto, R., Caputo, M., Arena, S., Caruso, P., Maiorino, M. I., & Esposito, K. (2022). Mediterranean Diet and Thyroid: An Interesting Alliance. *Nutrients, 14*(19). https://doi.org/10.3390/nu14194130

Capriello, S., Stramazzo, I., Bagaglini, M. F., Brusca, N., Virili, C., & Centanni, M. (2022). The relationship between thyroid disorders and vitamin A.: A narrative minireview. *Frontiers in endocrinology, 13*, 968215. https://doi.org/10.3389/fendo.2022.968215

Carazo, A., Macáková, K., Matoušová, K., Krčmová, L. K., Protti, M., & Mladěnka, P. (2021). Vitamin A Update: Forms, Sources, Kinetics, Detection, Function,

Deficiency, Therapeutic Use and Toxicity. *Nutrients, 13*(5). https://doi.org/10.3390/nu13051703

Carboni, L. (2022). Active Folate Versus Folic Acid: The Role of 5-MTHF (Methylfolate) in Human Health. *Integrative Medicine: A Clinician's Journal, 21*(3), 36-41. https://www.ncbi.nlm.nih.gov/pmc/articles/PMC9380836/

(2022, June 15). *MTHFR Gene, Folic Acid, and Preventing Neural Tube Defects.* Centers for Disease Control and Prevention. https://health.clevelandclinic.org/polyphenols

Cherayil B. J. (2010). Iron and immunity: immunological consequences of iron deficiency and overload. *Archivum immunologiae et therapiae experimentalis, 58*(6), 407–415. https://doi.org/10.1007/s00005-010-0095-9

Cleveland Clinic. (2023, August 15). *Foods Rich in Polyphenols — And Why They're Important.* Cleveland Clinic. https://health.clevelandclinic.org/polyphenols

Cleveland Clinic. *31 High-Fiber Foods You Should Be Eating.* Cleveland Clinic. https://health.clevelandclinic.org/high-fiber-foods

Ding, S., Jiang, H., & Fang, J. (2018). Regulation of Immune Function by Polyphenols. *Journal of Immunology Research, 2018.* https://doi.org/10.1155/2018/1264074

Dominguez, L. J., Farruggia, M., Veronese, N., & Barbagallo, M. (2021). Vitamin D Sources, Metabolism, and Deficiency: Available Compounds and Guidelines for Its Treatment. *Metabolites, 11*(4). https://doi.org/10.3390/metabo11040255

Doseděl, M., Jirkovský, E., Macáková, K., Krčmová, L. K., Javorská, L., Pourová, J., Mercolini, L., Remião, F., Nováková, L., Mladěnka, P., & OEMONOM, T. (2021). Vitamin C—Sources, Physiological Role, Kinetics, Deficiency, Use, Toxicity, and Determination. *Nutrients, 13*(2). https://doi.org/10.3390/nu13020615

Farasati Far, B., Behnoush, A. H., Ghondaghsaz, E., Habibi, M. A., & Khalaji, A. (2023). The interplay between vitamin C and thyroid. *Endocrinology, diabetes & metabolism, 6*(4), e432. https://doi.org/10.1002/edm2.432

Hanna, M., Jaqua, E., Nguyen, V., & Clay, J. (2022). B Vitamins: Functions and Uses in Medicine. *The Permanente Journal, 26*(2), 89-97. https://doi.org/10.7812/TPP/21.204

Hodges, R. E., & Minich, D. M. (2015). Modulation of Metabolic Detoxification Pathways Using Foods and Food-Derived Components: A Scientific Review with Clinical Application. *Journal of Nutrition and Metabolism, 2015.* https://doi.org/10.1155/2015/760689

Hollywood, J. B., Hutchinson, D., Feehery-Alpuerto, N., Whitfield, M., Davis, K., & Johnson, L. M. (2023).

The Effects of the Paleo Diet on Autoimmune Thyroid Disease: A Mixed Methods Review. *Journal of the American Nutrition Association, 42*(8), 727–736. https://doi.org/10.1080/27697061.2022.2159570

Knezevic, J., Starchl, C., Berisha, A. T., & Amrein, K. (2020). Thyroid-Gut-Axis: How Does the Microbiota Influence Thyroid Function? *Nutrients, 12*(6). https://doi.org/10.3390/nu12061769

Lebiedziński, F., & Lisowska, K. A. (2023). Impact of Vitamin D on Immunopathology of Hashimoto's Thyroiditis: From Theory to Practice. *Nutrients, 15*(14), 3174. https://doi.org/10.3390/nu15143174

(2024, April 15). *Selenium Fact Sheet for Health Professionals.* National Institutes of Health. https://ods.od.nih.gov/factsheets/Selenium-HealthProfessional/

(2022, September 28). *Zinc Fact Sheet for Health Professionals.* National Institutes of Health. https://ods.od.nih.gov/factsheets/zinc-healthprofessional/#:~:text=The%20richest%20food%20sources%20of%20zinc%20include%20meat%2C,dairy%20products%20also%20contain%20zinc%20%5B%203%20%5D

Roohani, N., Hurrell, R., Kelishadi, R., & Schulin, R. (2013). Zinc and its importance for human health: An integrative review. *Journal of Research in Medical Sciences : The Official Journal of Isfahan University of Medical Sciences, 18*(2), 144-157. https://www.ncbi.nlm.nih.gov/pmc/articles/PMC3724376/

Ruggeri, R. M., Barbalace, M. C., Croce, L., Malaguti, M., Campennì, A., Rotondi, M., Cannavò, S., & Hrelia, S. (2023). Autoimmune Thyroid Disorders: The Mediterranean Diet as a Protective Choice. *Nutrients*, *15*(18). https://doi.org/10.3390/nu15183953

Singh, V., Lee, G., Son, H., Koh, H., Kim, E. S., Unno, T., & Shin, H. (2022). Butyrate producers, "The Sentinel of Gut": Their intestinal significance with and beyond butyrate, and prospective use as microbial therapeutics. *Frontiers in Microbiology*, *13*. https://doi.org/10.3389/fmicb.2022.1103836

Sorrenti, S., Baldini, E., Pironi, D., Lauro, A., Tartaglia, F., Tripodi, D., Lori, E., Gagliardi, F., Praticò, M., Illuminati, G., Palumbo, P., & Ulisse, S. (2021). Iodine: Its Role in Thyroid Hormone Biosynthesis and Beyond. *Nutrients*, *13*(12). https://doi.org/10.3390/nu13124469

Stromsnes, K., Correas, A. G., Lehmann, J., Gambini, J., & Olaso-Gonzalez, G. (2021). Anti-Inflammatory Properties of Diet: Role in Healthy Aging. *Biomedicines*, *9*(8). https://doi.org/10.3390/biomedicines9080922

Ventura, M., Melo, M., & Carrilho, F. (2017). Selenium and Thyroid Disease: From Pathophysiology to Treatment. *International Journal of Endocrinology*, *2017*. https://doi.org/10.1155/2017/1297658

Wartenberg, L., MFA, RD, LD, & Spritzler, F. (2023, May 23). *Anti-Inflammatory Foods to Eat: A Full List.*

Healthline. https://www.healthline.com/nutrition/13-anti-inflammatory-foods#TOC_TITLE_HDR_

Yang, D., Wang, T., Long, M., & Li, P. (2020). Quercetin: Its Main Pharmacological Activity and Potential Application in Clinical Medicine. *Oxidative Medicine and Cellular Longevity, 2020.* https://doi.org/10.1155/2020/8825387

Chapter 7

Behan, C. (2020). The benefits of meditation and mindfulness practices during times of crisis such as COVID-19. *Irish Journal of Psychological Medicine*, 1-3. https://doi.org/10.1017/ipm.2020.38

Christie , J., ND, CNS (2022, August 15). *It's Time To Start Treating Coffee Like A Health Food.* Rupa Health. https://www.rupahealth.com/post/its-time-to-start-treating-coffee-like-a-health-food?utm_source=google&utm_medium=cpc&utm_campaign=pmax_20893116874&utm_content=&utm_term=&gad_source=1&gclid=Cj0KCQiA5-uuBhDzAR IsAAa21T_0YePAOrTHByv2FKrkGNa3j9z73DO6nn Tp3h_d9nKWe-qK1fK24z4aAk4BEALw_wcB

Ferrer-Cascales, R., Sánchez-SanSegundo, M., Ruiz-Robledillo, N., Albaladejo-Blázquez, N., Laguna-Pérez, A., & Zaragoza-Martí, A. (2018). Eat or Skip Breakfast? The Important Role of Breakfast Quality for Health-Related Quality of Life, Stress and Depression in Spanish Adolescents. *International Journal of*

Environmental Research and Public Health, 15(8). https://doi.org/10.3390/ijerph15081781

Green, M. E., Bernet, V., & Cheung, J. (2021). Thyroid Dysfunction and Sleep Disorders. *Frontiers in Endocrinology, 12.* https://doi.org/10.3389/fendo.2021.725829

Ikegami, K., Refetoff, S., Cauter, E. V., & Yoshimura, T. (2019). Interconnection between circadian clocks and thyroid function. *Nature Reviews. Endocrinology, 15*(10), 590. https://doi.org/10.1038/s41574-019-0237-z

Klasson, C. L., Sadhir, S., & Pontzer, H. (2022). Daily physical activity is negatively associated with thyroid hormone levels, inflammation, and immune system markers among men and women in the NHANES dataset. *PLoS ONE, 17*(7). https://doi.org/10.1371/journal.pone.0270221

Lim, J., & Hyun, J. (2021). The Impacts of Pilates and Yoga on Health-Promoting Behaviors and Subjective Health Status. *International Journal of Environmental Research and Public Health, 18*(7). https://doi.org/10.3390/ijerph18073802

Markomanolaki, Z. S., Tigani, X., Siamatras, T., Bacopoulou, F., Tsartsalis, A., Artemiadis, A., Megalooikonomou, V., Vlachakis, D., Chrousos, G. P., & Darviri, C. (2019). Stress Management in Women with Hashimoto's thyroiditis: A Randomized Controlled Trial. *Journal of Molecular Biochemistry,*

8(1), 3. https://www.ncbi.nlm.nih.gov/pmc/articles/PMC6688766/

Morris, C. J., Aeschbach, D., & Scheer, J. L. (2012). Circadian System, Sleep and Endocrinology. *Molecular and Cellular Endocrinology, 349*(1), 91. https://doi.org/10.1016/j.mce.2011.09.003

Mullur, R., Liu, Y., & Brent, G. A. (2014). Thyroid Hormone Regulation of Metabolism. *Physiological Reviews, 94*(2), 355-382. https://doi.org/10.1152/physrev.00030.2013

Worley, S. L. (2018). The Extraordinary Importance of Sleep: The Detrimental Effects of Inadequate Sleep on Health and Public Safety Drive an Explosion of Sleep Research. *Pharmacy and Therapeutics, 43*(12), 758-763. https://www.ncbi.nlm.nih.gov/pmc/articles/PMC6281147/

Chapter 8

Dube, Shanta R. PhD, MPH; Fairweather, DeLisa PhD; Pearson, William S. PhD, MHA; Felitti, Vincent J. MD; Anda, Robert F. MD, MS; Croft, Janet B. PhD. Cumulative Childhood Stress and Autoimmune Diseases in Adults. Psychosomatic Medicine 71(2):p 243-250, February 2009. | DOI: 10.1097/PSY.0b013e3181907888

Mizokami, T., Wu Li, A., El-Kaissi, S., & Wall, J. R. (2004). Stress and thyroid autoimmunity. *Thyroid : official journal of the American Thyroid Association, 14*(12), 1047–1055. https://doi.org/10.1089/thy.2004.14.1047

(2022, October 4). *Adopting healthy habits: What do we know about the science of behavior change?* National Institute on Aging. https://www.nia.nih.gov/news/adopting-healthy-habits-what-do-we-know-about-science-behavior-change

(2020, November). *Changing Your Habits for Better Health.* National Institute of Diabetes and Digestive and Kidney Diseases. https://www.niddk.nih.gov/health-information/diet-nutrition/changing-habits-better-health

ACKNOWLEDGMENTS

*T*here are so many people who have crossed my path and have become a part of my health journey. Some came as a healer, a mentor, a friend, or a colleague. You never really know what your words or acts of kindness truly mean to someone. All of you have been influential people in *my life* and have made waves of difference, and for that, I am forever grateful!

My husband, Joseph—in sickness and in health, in good times and in bad, your unconditional love and your unwavering support and belief in me and my ambitious dreams have meant the absolute world! You are my greatest adventure. <3

My fellow health and wellness friends and experts—Taylor Knese, Layne VanLieshout, Aliesha Mann, Emily Burger, Marketta Moore, Krissy Ford, Rachel Genz, Sarah Mathis, Trisha Zehrung, Jamie Javed, Laura DeCesaris and Jade Etter. Thank you for supporting me and my own health and wellness business, whether as friends, mentors, or both. We are definitely not meant to do this work alone, and you ladies have made it so much more enjoyable! Keep spreading your light. Keep showing up in BIG ways. Keep IMPACTING the world through medicine, because the work you are doing to serve others is UNDENIABLE. If you are looking for a Holistic Health Consultant/Coach, please check out these wonderful ladies!

My OG mentor and real-life badass, Bonnie C., thank you for being the *first* person to really push me to step into the leader I know I can be. You said, "You don't have to know everything. You just have to know where your resources are." It's a simple yet powerful sentence, and it truly gave me, and still gives me, the courage to push through my fears when it comes to taking the next BIG step.

My former nursing manager, Tom J., thank you for making me feel seen as a human. You are an incredible leader, and anyone who gets the chance to have you as a boss or friend is truly blessed.

Of course, thank you to my *amazing* chiropractor, Jodi C. DC, CACCP. You are a *master* in your work, you care about your patients' well-being, and you are someone who has taken a part in *dramatically changing* my life. Thank you for being an amazing human!

Thank you to my one and only Functional Medicine doctor. You connected the dots for me, you cared about my outcome, and you helped me to heal so that I could do the same for others. You have changed the trajectory in which I practice medicine, and I am forever grateful. Thank you for healing me and helping me align with my purpose!

Thank you to this wonderful human being, Melanie R., MS, LPCC, LMFT, who has walked alongside me for years, helping me to heal and recognize that I am *worthy*.

Thank you to Dr. Izabella Wentz for being an incredible pioneer in the Hashimoto's world and inspiring women worldwide to take control of their thyroid health.

To my amazing editing team and publishing team, THANK YOU so much for the amazing work that you do and helping to bring my story to life!

AUTHOR BIO

*M*eet Jasmine! She is a dedicated wife and proud dog mom to a lively 3 year-old german shepherd. Outside of her work she embodies a profound appreciation for life's simple joys! Fuelled by a deep-seated love for knowledge, she is rarely seen without a book in hand, favoring insightful health and wellness and the occasional captivating romance trilogy. She indulges in meditation, yoga, pilates, hiking, and channeling her inner artist through painting. With the spirit of adventure, she loves to travel, embracing new cultures, history, food, and experiences.

A multifaceted force in the world of health and wellness- Jasmine is a Functional Medicine Certified Health Coach, Registered Nurse, Hashimoto's educator, advocate, and patient, and the founder of Love, Your Thyroid™. She embodies a deep-rooted passion for medicine and a relentless dedication to helping others. She has had a passion for medicine and helping others from an early age, and it was her personal struggle with autoimmune thyroid issues that ultimately ignited her mission.

Her mission is simple: to bridge the gap in Hashimoto's care and empower women to take control of their thyroid health.

It's time to *do something different*. Conventional solutions just *aren't enough*. Hashimoto's care goes *beyond simply medicating* the thyroid. It *requires* a whole-body approach to get to the root cause(s) of your autoimmune disease, identify and remove your unique triggers, and make the necessary lifestyle changes to be able to *live a vibrant life in remission*. It't time to come back to loving your thyroid, friend!

Love, Your Thyroid™ –your go-to resource hub for all things Hashimoto's. Imagine a life where Hashimoto's doesn't control you but you control it!

I cant wait to help support you inside! Join now by going to the link below.

jasmineparkercoaching.com/loveyourthyroid

Helping YOU heal YOU!

URGENT PLEA!

Thank you for reading my book!

I appreciate all of your feedback and
I love hearing what you have to say.

I need your input to make the next version of this
book and my future books better.

Please take a hot second to leave a helpful review on
Amazon, let me know what you think of the book!

Thanks so much!

Jasmine Parker